Dedication

To my wife, whose support and encouragement made this book possible.
—Harry Mcintosh

Message from the
Publisher

WELCOME TO OUR NERVOUS SYSTEM

Some people say that the World Wide Web is a graphical extension of the information superhighway, just a network of humans and machines sending each other long lists of the equivalent of digital junk mail.

I think it is much more than that. To me, the Web is nothing less than the nervous system of the entire planet—not just a collection of computer brains connected together, but more like a billion silicon neurons entangled and recirculating electrochemical signals of information and data, each contributing to the birth of another CPU and another Web site.

Think of each person's hard disk connected at once to every other hard disk on earth, driven by human navigators searching like Columbus for the New World. Seen this way the Web is more of a super entity, a growing, living thing, controlled by the universal human will to expand, to be more. Yet, unlike a purposeful business plan with rigid rules, the Web expands in a nonlinear, unpredictable, creative way that echoes natural evolution.

We created our Web site not just to extend the reach of our computer book products but to be part of this synaptic neural network, to experience, like a nerve in the body, the flow of ideas and then to pass those ideas up the food chain of the mind. Your mind. Even more, we wanted to pump some of our own creative juices into this rich wine of technology.

TASTE OUR DIGITAL WINE

And so we ask you to taste our wine by visiting the body of our business. Begin by understanding the metaphor we have created for our Web site—a universal learning center, situated in outer space in the form of a space station. A place where you can journey to study any topic from the convenience of your own screen. Right now we are focusing on computer topics, but the stars are the limit on the Web.

If you are interested in discussing this Web site or finding out more about the Waite Group, please send me e-mail with your comments, and I will be happy to respond. Being a programmer myself, I love to talk about technology and find out what our readers are looking for.

Sincerely,

Mitchell Waite

Mitchell Waite, C.E.O. and Publisher

200 Tamal Plaza
Corte Madera, CA 94925
415-924-2575
415-924-2576 fax

Web site:
http://www.waite.com/waite

CREATING THE HIGHEST QUALITY COMPUTER BOOKS IN THE INDUSTRY

Waite Group Press
Waite Group New Media

Come Visit
WAITE.COM
Waite Group Press
World Wide Web Site

Now find all the latest information on Waite Group books at our new Web site, **http://www.waite.com/waite.** You'll find an online catalog where you can examine and order any title, review upcoming books, and send e-mail to our authors and editors. Our FTP site has all you need to update your book: the latest program listings, errata sheets, most recent versions of Fractint, POV Ray, Polyray, DMorph, and all the programs featured in our books. So download, talk to us, and ask questions on **http://www.waite.com/waite.**

The New Arrivals Room has all our new books listed by month. Just click for a description, Index, Table of Contents, and links to authors.

The Backlist Room has all our books listed alphabetically.

The People Room is where you'll interact with Waite Group employees.

Links to Cyberspace get you in touch with other computer book publishers and other interesting Web sites.

The FTP site contains all program listings, errata sheets, etc.

The Order Room is where you can order any of our books online.

The Subject Room contains typical book pages which show description, Index, Table of Contents, and links to authors.

World Wide Web:

COME SURF OUR TURF—THE WAITE GROUP WEB

http://www.waite.com/waite
Gopher: gopher.waite.com
FTP: ftp.waite.com

About the Author

Harry Mcintosh has been hopelessly enmeshed in computers since receiving a B.A. in computer science from the University of Colorado at Boulder in 1978. Since then he has worked on a wide variety of different operating systems, languages, and applications—everything from assembly language on microcomputers to PL/I on mainframes. In recent years, he has focused on writing cross-platform applications for personal computers. He runs PAC Software, a small consulting firm based in Denver, Colorado.

Table of Contents

Contents

VIII

IX

XI

XIII

XIV

Introduction

Welcome to *Talk Java™ to Me*.

You may think you're holding a book in your hand. Well, you are. But you're also holding a CD-ROM, and it's the real key to *Talk Java™ to Me* because *it* will teach you Java™. Most books on Java include a CD-ROM, and often they just contain a few examples of Java programs and maybe the Java Developer's Kit. This CD-ROM contains much more—a complete, multimedia tutorial to Java. Hidden inside the CD-ROM are two narrators who will teach you Java by talking to you. As they explain the concepts of the language, animated text and graphics on the screen will illustrate what they are saying. It's simply the fastest, easiest way to learn Java.

The first thing the CD-ROM will do when you run it is ask some questions about your background. It will ask if you know C, C++, HTML, object-oriented programming, and some other things. Based on the answers you give to these questions, it will *customize* the tutorial for you. Almost every lesson on the CD-ROM will be customized in this way. That means you can use it whether you know C++ or not. It also means the CD-ROM will cover topics you need, without covering those you don't need.

The CD-ROM and the book are designed to be used together. You use the CD-ROM to learn Java and the book as a reference tool to look up specific details as you write Java programs. The book also includes exercises for you to do after finishing each lesson on the CD-ROM.

CD-ROM Lessons 1, 2, and 3—Introduction

The CD-ROM begins by teaching the basics of the Java language. If you know C or C++, it will do this by comparing Java to C or C++. If you don't know them, don't worry—it will teach Java to you from the ground up, without mentioning C or C++. In either case, after you finish these lessons you'll know enough about Java to start writing simple programs.

CD-ROM Lesson 4—Applets

This lesson starts with one of the most important—and most fun—aspects of Java: writing applets for Web pages. It covers the structure of applets, how to draw on the screen, and how to respond to events like clicking the mouse and typing on the keyboard. If you don't know HTML, it will provide a brief introduction to HTML. Whether you know HTML or not, it will show you how to use HTML to include an applet on your Web page.

CD-ROM Lesson 5—Animation and Threads

Many applets are used to bring a Web page alive by providing animation. This lesson shows how to do that. This includes how (and when) to use double-buffering to reduce animation flicker and how to create threads to process the animation.

CD-ROM Lesson 6—Applications

Java is often used to create applets for Web pages, but that's not all it can do. It can also be a full-fledged application language, like C++ or BASIC. With it, you can write applications which not only perform the same processing as other languages, but also that can be run on any Java platform—Windows, Macintosh, or UNIX.

Lesson 6 explains the basic structure of Java applications. It also describes how to create and manage windows and menus from a Java application.

CD-ROM Lesson 7—Dialogs

Lesson 7 shows how to add dialog boxes to your applications. This includes using layout managers to control the placement and sizing of controls and dialog boxes.

CD-ROM Lesson 8—Controls

After you learn how to create dialog boxes in Lesson 7, you'll want to know all about the controls you can use in Java. This lesson covers that—everything from the simple push button to the more complicated scroll bar.

CD-ROM Lessons 9 and 10—Advanced Language

In Lessons 1, 2, and 3, the CD-ROM covered the basics of the Java language. Lessons 9 and 10 cover some more advanced aspects of the language, including topics like exception handling, data conversion, the "equals" operator, packages, access control, interfaces, abstract classes, multi-threading, and synchronization.

CD-ROM Lesson 11—Standard Classes

Lessons 4 through 8 showed how to use many of the standard classes that are part of Java. This lesson covers the rest of them—including file i/o, networking, hash tables, vectors, stacks, and more.

Book Chapter 1—Using the CD-ROM

This brief chapter explains how to install and use the CD-ROM.

Book Chapters 2 and 3—Exercises

These chapters provide exercises for you to do at the end of each lesson on the CD-ROM. Answers to the exercises are also included.

Book Chapters 4, 5, and 6—Java Reference

These chapters provide a reference tool for the Java language. Forget the syntax of the *for* statement? Just look it up here. Forget what access is provided by the *protected* keyword? That's here too. These chapters are a quick and easy way to refresh your memory about Java as you are writing Java programs.

Book Chapter 7—Standard Java Classes

Java includes a lot of standard classes which let you do everything from draw graphics in an applet to read text from a file. This chapter lists these classes and explains how to use them. After you learn the basics from listening to the CD-ROM, this chapter provides a simple way to find the details you'll need as you are programming.

PART I

CD-ROM Companion

CHAPTER 1

Getting Started

You probably think you're holding a book in your hand. Well, that's true...sort of. But *Talk Java™ to Me* isn't just a book—it isn't even *mainly* a book. It also includes a multimedia CD-ROM, and the CD-ROM will teach you Java™.

You see, hiding on the CD-ROM are two narrators. When you run the CD-ROM, they will teach Java by *talking* to you. That's the real key to learning Java—hearing a couple of people just *explain* it to you. Hearing is a very powerful way to learn, and *Talk Java™ to Me* taps that power to get you up and going in Java quickly and easily.

While the narrators are talking, animated text and graphics on the screen will illustrate what they're saying. Having those two things happening at once—hearing a voice and watching graphics—is a great combination. There's just no better way to learn.

Of course, the book plays an important part too. After each lesson on the CD-ROM, you'll use exercises from Chapter 2 of the book. There are answers to those exercises in Chapter 3. The rest of the book provides a reference for Java. It's a handy way to refresh your memory about a detail you need to know while you're doing the exercises—and later when you're writing Java programs.

Running the CD-ROM

Running the CD is very simple. If you're using Windows 3.1 (or Windows NT 3.51), look at the CD-ROM using the File Manager. It will look like Figure 1-1. Just double-click on the JAVA.EXE icon, and you'll be up and running.

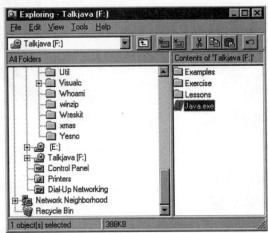

Figure 1-1 The CD-ROM viewed with File Manager

If you're using Windows 95 (or Windows NT 4.0), use the Explorer to look at the CD-ROM. It will look like Figure 1-2. Run *Talk Java™ to Me* by double-clicking on the JAVA.EXE icon.

The first time you run the CD-ROM, it will know you're just starting out, so it will automatically start with Lesson 1. It will also create a very small file that is named TALKJAVA.DAT in your WINDOWS directory.

4

When you run the CD-ROM from then on, it will always start out by asking who you are. It does that by displaying either the dialog box shown in Figure 1-3, or the one shown in Figure 1-4. It needs to know who you are so it can start up where you left off last time. It also needs to know who you are because the content of the CD is customized based on your background (whether you know C, C++, HTML, etc.).

That's all there is to it. So get to it—put down this book and crank up the CD-ROM.

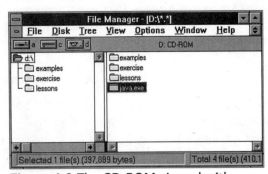

Figure 1-2 The CD-ROM viewed with Explorer

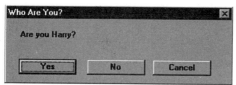

Figure 1-3 The CD-ROM asking who you are

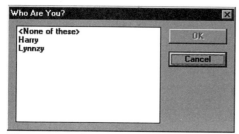

Figure 1-4 The CD-ROM asking who you are

Installing the Java Compiler

Before you can start writing Java programs, you'll need a Java compiler. There are several available, including one from SunSoft named the Java Developer's Kit (JDK). SunSoft's JDK is available for various platforms; we've put the one for Windows NT/95 on the CD. (As of the writing of this book, a JDK for Windows 3.1 is not available.)

If you are using a Java compiler you have obtained from elsewhere, that's fine—you don't need to install the one from the CD, too.

If you want to install the copy from the CD, begin by copying \COMPILE\JDK.EXE from the CD to your hard drive. You should probably copy it to the root of your hard drive. That means you'll end up with a directory named JAVA in the root directory. If you prefer to have Java in another directory, copy JDK.EXE to that directory.

Now just run JDK.EXE. It will unpack the Java Developer's Kit. To use it, be sure the BIN directory it creates is in your search path.

CHAPTER 2

Exercises

After completing each lesson on the CD-ROM, you should complete the exercises for that lesson. Answers to the exercises can be found in Chapter 3.

LESSON 1

Introduction

> **ABOUT THE LESSON 1 EXERCISES**
>
> You should do different exercises for Lesson 1 depending upon your background. If you know C++, you should do Exercises 1, 3, and 4. If you don't know C++, but you know C, you should do Exercises 1 and 3. If you don't know either C or C++, you should do Exercises 1 and 2.

Exercise 1

Look on the CD-ROM in directory \EXERCISE\01. It contains a simple Java™ application that performs a numeric calculation and prints the results. Copy the program to your hard drive then compile and run it.

Exercise 2

Modify the application you used in Exercise 1 so it calculates the sum of 1.23, 55, and 93.82.

Exercise 3

Write an application that adds together the integers from 1 to 100, excluding from the total any integers that are even multiples of 3 or 10. Display the resulting sum.

Exercise 4

Write a class to handle dates. The class should include two constructors—one that has no parameters and assigns a default date, and one that has three parameters for the day, month, and year. The class should also have two methods. The first method should add a given number of days to the date, and the second should compare two dates and return true if they are the same, and false if not.

Write an application (i.e., another class that includes a *main* method) to test the date class.

LESSON 2

Java Language

Exercise 5

Write an application that adds together the integers from 1 to 100. Do it first using a `while` loop and then using a `for` loop. Display the resulting sum.

Exercise 6

Modify the application from Exercise 5 to exclude from the sum any integers that are even multiples of 3 and to add twice any integers that are even multiples of 10.

Exercise 7

Write an application that assigns a value to *b* depending upon the value of *a*. Use a switch statement to do this. If *a* is either 5 or 6, *b* should be set to 1. If *a* is 7, *b* should be set to 2. If *a* has any other value, *b* should be set to 0. Oh, and while you're at it, set *c* to 8 if *a* is 7, and set *d* to 8 if *a* isn't 5, 6, or 7.

LESSON 3

Classes

Exercise 8

Write a class to handle employees. The class should keep track of each employee's name, hourly wage, and the number of hours worked in the most recent pay period. Include in the class a method that calculates the current gross pay (i.e., the wage times the number of hours worked).

Write an application (i.e., another class that includes a *main* method) that uses the employee class to create a couple of employees. Assign names, wages, and hours to each of the employees. Calculate and output the gross pay for each employee.

Exercise 9

Modify the class written in Exercise 8 to include two constructors. The first constructor should have a single parameter: the employee's name. It should set the wage to a default value and the hours to zero. The second constructor should have three parameters: the name, wage, and current hours.

Modify your *main* method to use the two constructors.

Exercise 10

Modify the class written in Exercise 9 to include a new method. It should set the hours worked by one employee to those worked by another. (This might be used, for example, to set the hours for all the members of a crew to the hours entered for one member of that crew.)

Modify your *main* method to use the new method.

LESSON 4

Applets

Exercise 11

Write an applet method that draws lines that can be of any thickness. (Hint: You'll have to do this by drawing several lines next to each other; each of the lines you draw will be just one pixel wide.) The parameters to this method should include the starting point for the line, the ending point for the line, and the width of the line.

Write a similar applet method that will draw ovals with a border of any width.

Test the two methods by writing an applet that draws several of the thick lines and ellipses. Draw the graphics in red.

Exercise 12

Modify the applet from Exercise 11 to draw a 5-pixel-thick *X* and a 5-pixel-thick *O*. The *X* and *O* should be centered in the middle of the applet's area. If the user clicks the mouse inside the applet, the *X* should be moved to the position of the mouse click. The next time the mouse is clicked, the *O* should be moved. Continue alternating between moving the *X* and moving the *O*.

LESSON 5

Animation and Threads

Exercise 13

Write an applet that allows you to add a scrolling marquee to a Web page. By a scrolling marquee, I mean a bit of text that scrolls from right to left inside a rectangle. The text will start on the right-hand side of the rectangle and eventually disappear on the left-hand side. Make the text animation smooth by using double-buffering.

LESSON 6

Frames and Menus

Exercise 14

Write an application that displays a frame. Inside that frame, draw a 200-pixel by 200-pixel square. Inside the square, draw a line from the upper left-hand corner to the lower right-hand corner. Draw another line from the upper right-hand corner to the lower left-hand corner. Draw a small rectangle centered in the square.

Exercise 15

Modify the application from Exercise 14 to include a menu. It should have a File menu with one entry: Exit. It should have a Shape menu with two entries: Oval and Rectangle. If you pick the Exit entry, the program should end. If you pick one of the Shape entries, it should change the shape in the center of the square to either an oval or a rectangle.

LESSON 7

Dialogs

Exercise 16

Modify the application from Exercise 15 to include Choose as a third entry on the Shape menu. If the user picks that entry, a dialog box should be displayed. The dialog should have two buttons, labeled Oval and Rectangle. When the user presses one of the buttons, the dialog should disappear, and the shape in the frame should be modified to either an oval or a rectangle.

Exercise 17

Write an application that displays a dialog box. The box should have two rows of buttons. The first row should have two buttons, labeled A and B, each of which should occupy half the width of the row. The second row should have four buttons, labeled 1, 2, 3, and 4, each of which should occupy one quarter of the row. Use the GridBagLayout manager to do this.

LESSON 8

Controls

Exercise 18

Write an application that draws a red circle in its frame. Include in the frame a menu entry named Dialog. When the user selects that entry, display a dialog box. The box should contain: (1) a Choice control that allows the user to select either Red or Green; (2) two group Checkbox controls that allow the user to select Circle or Square; and (3) an OK button. After the user finishes using the dialog box, redraw the frame using the circle and shape selected by the user.

Exercise 19

Write an application that displays the letters *A* through *Z*, each on a separate line, in a panel inside a frame. Include a scrollbar in the panel. Use the scrollbar to scroll the display. Here's a hint: Create a **String** object like this:

```
String alpha = "ABCDEFGHIJKLMNOPQRSTUVWXYZ";
```

Select the letter to be displayed with:

```
alpha.substring(2,3);
```

The above line will select the third character in **alpha**.

LESSON 9

Advanced Language

Exercise 20

Write a class that keeps track of a tic-tac-toe board. The class should include a method that lets you clear the board, a method that determines if either *X* or *O* has won the game, and a method that lets you set a particular position on the board to either *X* or

O. The method that lets you set a position should check to see if the position is already occupied and should throw an exception if it is.

Use the tic-tac-toe class to write an applet that lets two people play tic-tac-toe.

LESSON 10
More Advanced Language

Exercise 21

Create a package that has three classes: one for dates, one for times, and one for dates and times. Use the appropriate keyword for each field variable to ensure that a user of the classes cannot change the field variables directly—they should be changed only by calling methods in the classes.

Write an application that tests the package.

LESSON 11
Standard Java Classes

Exercise 22

Write an application that reads a text file (the input file) and creates a new text file (the output file). The output file should contain the same text as the input file, except that all occurrences of the letter *a* should be replaced with the letter *b*.

Exercise 23

Write an application that reads an HTML file from the Internet and reports the number of occurrences of the letter *a* in the file.

CHAPTER 3

Answers to Exercises

Exercise 2

```
class first {
    public static void main(String param[]) {
        double sum;
        sum = 1.23 + 55 + 93.82;
        System.out.println(sum);
    }
}
```

13

Exercise 3

```
class sum {
    public static void main(String param[]) {
        int i;
        int sum=0;
        for (i=1; i<=100; ++i) {
            if ( (i%3 != 0) && (i%10 != 0) ) {
                sum += i;
            }
        }
        System.out.println("The sum is:");
        System.out.println(sum);
    }
}
```

Exercise 4

```
/* This class should be in file "test.java". */

import date;

class test {
    public static void main(String param[]) {
        date d1 = new date();
        date d2 = new date(2010,5,20);
        d1.year = 2010;
        d1.month = 4;
        d1.day = 30;
        d1.addDays(20);
        if (d1.isEqual(d2)) {
            System.out.println("The dates are equal");
        } else {
            System.out.println("The dates are unequal");
        }
    }
}


/* This class should be in file "date.java". */

class date {

    int year;
    int month;
    int day;

    date() {
        year = 2000;
        month = 1;
        day = 1;
    }

    date(int year,int month,int day) {
        this.year = year;
        this.month = month;
        this.day = day;
    }

    /*** Add the given number of days to the date ***/
    void addDays(int days) {
        int daysInMonths[] = {31, 28, 31, 30, 31, 30, 31, 31, 30, 31, 30, 31};
        day += days;
        daysInMonths[1] = 28 + (leapYear() ? 1 : 0);
        while (day > daysInMonths[month-1]) {
            day -= daysInMonths[month-1];
            if (++month > 12) {
                month = 1;
                ++year;
                daysInMonths[1] = 28 + (leapYear() ? 1 : 0);
            }
        }
    }
}
```

14

```
    /*** Determine if the date is for a leap year ***/
    boolean leapYear() {
        if ( (year % 100) == 0) {
            if ( (year % 400) == 0) {
                return true;
            } else {
                return false;
            }
        } else {
            if ( (year % 4) == 0) {
                return true;
            } else {
                return false;
            }
        }
    }

    /*** Determine if two dates are equal ***/
    boolean isEqual(date d) {
        if (year != d.year) return false;
        if (month != d.month) return false;
        if (day != d.day) return false;
        return true;
    }
}
```

Exercise 5

```
class add {
    public static void main(String param[]) {

        int sum1 = 0;
        int sum2 = 0;
        int i;

        i = 1;
        while (i <= 100) {
            sum1 += i;
            ++i;
        }

        for (i=1; i<=100; ++i) {
            sum2 += i;
        }

        System.out.println("The answers are:");
        System.out.println(sum1);
        System.out.println(sum2);

    }
}
```

Exercise 6

```
class add {
    public static void main(String param[]) {

        int sum1 = 0;
        int sum2 = 0;
        int i;

        i = 1;
        while (i <= 100) {
            if ( (i%3) != 0) {
                if ( (i%10) == 0) {
                    sum1 += i;
                }
                sum1 += i;
            }
            ++i;
        }

        for (i=1; i<=100; ++i) {
            if ( (i%3) == 0) {
                continue;
            }
            if ( (i%10) == 0) {
                sum2 += i;
            }
            sum2 += i;
        }

        System.out.println("The answers are:");
        System.out.println(sum1);
        System.out.println(sum2);

    }
}
```

16

Exercise 7

```
class branch {
    public static void main(String param[]) {
        int a = 5; // Test different values here.
        int b = 0;
        int c = 0;
        int d = 0;

        switch (a) {

        case 5:
        case 6:
            b = 1;
            break;
```

```
        case 7:
            b = 2;
            c = 8;
            break;

        default:
            b = 0;
            d = 8;
            break;
        }

        System.out.println("b, c, and d are:");
        System.out.println(b);
        System.out.println(c);
        System.out.println(d);
    }
}
```

Exercises 8, 9, and 10

```
/*** This class should be in file "testemp.java" ***/

class testemp {
    public static void main(String param[]) {
        employee e1 = new employee("Joachim");
        employee e2 = new employee("Mitchell",40,50);

        e1.getHours(e2);

        float pay1 = e1.pay();
        float pay2 = e2.pay();

        System.out.println(pay1);
        System.out.println(pay2);
    }
}

/*** This class should be in file "employee.java" ***/

class employee {

    String name;
    float wage;
    float hours;

    employee(String n) {
        name = n;
        wage = 70;
        hours = 0;
    }
```

17

continued on next page

continued from previous page

```java
    employee(String n,float w,float h) {
        name = n;
        wage = w;
        hours = h;
    }

    void getHours(employee e) {
        hours = e.hours;
    }

    float pay() {
        return hours * wage;
    }
}
```

Exercise 11

```java
/*** The following should be in "thick.html" ***/

<html>
<body>
<applet code="thick" width=200 height=200>
</applet>
</body>
</html>

/*** The following should be in "thick.java" ***/

import java.awt.*;
import java.applet.Applet;

public class thick extends Applet {

    public void paint(Graphics g) {
        g.setColor(Color.red);
        thickLine(g,5,40,size().width-5,size().height-40,5);
        thickLine(g,40,5,size().width-40,size().height-5,5);
        thickOval(g,40,40,size().width-80,size().height-80,5);
    }

    void thickLine(Graphics g,int x1,int y1,int x2,int y2,int thickness) {
        int height;
        int i;
        boolean mostlyHorizontal;
        int width;

        height = y2 - y1;
        if (height < 0) height = -height;
        width = x2 - x1;
        if (width < 0) width = -width;
        if (width > height) {
            mostlyHorizontal = true;
        } else {
            mostlyHorizontal = false;
        }
```

```
        for (i=0; i<thickness; ++i) {
            if (mostlyHorizontal) {
                g.drawLine(x1,y1+i,x2,y2+i);
            } else {
                g.drawLine(x1+i,y1,x2+i,y2);
            }
        }
    }

    void thickOval(Graphics g,int x,int y,int width,int height,int thickness) {
        int i;

        for (i=0; i<thickness; ++i) {
            g.drawOval(x+i,y+i,width-(2*i),height-(2*i));
        }
    }
}
```

Exercise 12

```
/*** The following should be in "xando.html" ***/

<html>
<body>
<applet code="xando" width=400 height=400>
</applet>
</body>
</html>

/*** The following should be in "xando.java" ***/

import java.awt.*;
import java.applet.Applet;

public class xando extends Applet {

    boolean xTurn;
    int xAtX;
    int xAtY;
    int oAtX;
    int oAtY;

    public void init() {
        xTurn = true;
        xAtX = size().width/2;
        xAtY = size().height/2;
        oAtX = size().width/2;
        oAtY = size().height/2;
    }

    public void paint(Graphics g) {
        g.setColor(Color.red);
        thickLine(g,xAtX-40,xAtY-40,xAtX+40,xAtY+40,5);
```

19

continued on next page

continued from previous page

```
            thickLine(g,xAtX-40,xAtY+40,xAtX+40,xAtY-40,5);
            thickOval(g,oAtX-40,oAtY-40,80,80,5);
    }

    public boolean mouseDown(Event e,int x,int y) {
        if (xTurn) {
            xAtX = x;
            xAtY = y;
            xTurn = false;
        } else {
            oAtX = x;
            oAtY = y;
            xTurn = true;
        }
        repaint();
        return true;
    }

    void thickLine(Graphics g,int x1,int y1,int x2,int y2,int thickness) {
        int height;
        int i;
        boolean mostlyHorizontal;
        int width;

        height = y2 - y1;
        if (height < 0) height = -height;
        width = x2 - x1;
        if (width < 0) width = -width;
        if (width > height) {
            mostlyHorizontal = true;
        } else {
            mostlyHorizontal = false;
        }

        for (i=0; i<thickness; ++i) {
            if (mostlyHorizontal) {
                g.drawLine(x1,y1+i,x2,y2+i);
            } else {
                g.drawLine(x1+i,y1,x2+i,y2);
            }
        }
    }

    void thickOval(Graphics g,int x,int y,int width,int height,int thickness) {
        int i;

        for (i=0; i<thickness; ++i) {
            g.drawOval(x+i,y+i,width-(2*i),height-(2*i));
        }
    }
}
```

Exercise 13

```java
import java.awt.*;
import java.applet.Applet;

public class ticker extends Applet implements Runnable {
    Image offScreenImage;
    Graphics offScreenGraphics;
    int textAt;
    Thread thread;
    String text;
    FontMetrics fm;

    public void init() {
        offScreenImage = createImage(size().width, size().height);
        offScreenGraphics = offScreenImage.getGraphics();
        textAt = size().width;
        text = getParameter("text");
        if (text == null) {
            text = "Waite Group Press";
        }
        thread = new Thread(this);
        thread.start();
    }

    public void update(Graphics g) {
        paint(offScreenGraphics);
        g.drawImage(offScreenImage, 0, 0, null);
    }

    public void paint(Graphics g) {
        fm = g.getFontMetrics();
        g.setColor(getBackground());
        g.fillRect(0,0,size().width,size().height);
        g.setColor(Color.red);
        textAt -= 5;
        if (textAt < -fm.stringWidth(text)) {
            textAt = size().width;
        }
        g.drawString(text,textAt,
            (size().height-fm.getAscent()+fm.getDescent())/2+fm.getAscent());
    }

    public void stop() {
        thread.stop();
    }

    public void run() {
        for (;;) {
            repaint();
            try { thread.sleep(50); }
            catch (Exception e) { return; }
        }
    }
}
```

21

Exercises 14 and 15

```java
/*** The following should be in "shape.java" ***/

import java.awt.*;
import shapeFrame;

public class shape {

    public static void main(String[] param) {
        new shapeFrame();
    }

}

/*** The following should be in "shapeFrame.java" ***/

import java.awt.*;

class shapeFrame extends Frame {

    boolean displayRectangle;
    int drawingWidth;
    int drawingHeight;

    public shapeFrame() {
        super("Shape");
        displayRectangle = true;
        MenuBar bar = new MenuBar();
        Menu menu1 = new Menu("File");
        menu1.add("Exit");
        bar.add(menu1);
        Menu menu2 = new Menu("Shape");
        menu2.add("Rectangle");
        menu2.add("Oval");
        bar.add(menu2);
        setMenuBar(bar);
        drawingHeight = 200;
        drawingWidth = 200;
        resize(drawingWidth+20,drawingHeight+100);
        show();
    }

    public boolean handleEvent(Event event) {
        if (event.id == Event.WINDOW_DESTROY) {
            return action(event,"Exit");
        } else {
            return super.handleEvent(event);
        }
    }

    public boolean action(Event event,Object what) {
        if (what == "Exit") {
            System.exit(0);
            return true;
```

22

```
        } else if (what == "Rectangle") {
            displayRectangle = true;
            repaint();
            return true;
        } else if (what == "Oval") {
            displayRectangle = false;
            repaint();
            return true;
        }
        return false;
    }

    public void paint(Graphics g) {
        g.setColor(Color.black);
        g.drawRect(0,0,drawingWidth,drawingHeight);
        g.drawLine(0,0,drawingWidth,drawingHeight);
        g.drawLine(drawingWidth,0,0,drawingHeight);
        g.setColor(Color.red);
        if (displayRectangle) {
            g.fillRect(drawingWidth/2-20,drawingHeight/2-20,40,40);
        } else {
            g.fillOval(drawingWidth/2-20,drawingHeight/2-20,40,40);
        }
    }

}
```

Exercise 16

```
/*** The following should be in "shape.java" ***/

import java.awt.*;
import shapeFrame;

public class shape {

    public static void main(String[] param) {
        new shapeFrame();
    }

}

/*** The following should be in "shapeFrame.java" ***/

import java.awt.*;
import shapeDialog;

class shapeFrame extends Frame {

    boolean displayRectangle;
    int drawingWidth;
    int drawingHeight;
```

continued on next page

continued from previous page

```
    public shapeFrame() {
        super("Shape");
        displayRectangle = true;
        MenuBar bar = new MenuBar();
        Menu menu1 = new Menu("File");
        menu1.add("Exit");
        bar.add(menu1);
        Menu menu2 = new Menu("Shape");
        menu2.add("Rectangle");
        menu2.add("Oval");
        menu2.add("Choose");
        bar.add(menu2);
        setMenuBar(bar);
        drawingHeight = 200;
        drawingWidth = 200;
        resize(drawingWidth+20,drawingHeight+100);
        show();
    }

    public boolean handleEvent(Event event) {
        if (event.id == Event.WINDOW_DESTROY) {
            if (event.target == this) {
                return action(event,"Exit");
            }
        }
        return super.handleEvent(event);
    }

    public boolean action(Event event,Object what) {
        if (what == "Exit") {
            System.exit(0);
            return true;
        } else if (what == "Rectangle") {
            displayRectangle = true;
            repaint();
            return true;
        } else if (what == "Oval") {
            displayRectangle = false;
            repaint();
            return true;
        } else if (what == "Choose") {
            new shapeDialog(this);
            return true;
        }
        return false;
    }

    public void paint(Graphics g) {
        g.setColor(Color.black);
        g.drawRect(0,0,drawingWidth,drawingHeight);
```

24

```
        g.drawLine(0,0,drawingWidth,drawingHeight);
        g.drawLine(drawingWidth,0,0,drawingHeight);
        g.setColor(Color.red);
        if (displayRectangle) {
            g.fillRect(drawingWidth/2-20,drawingHeight/2-20,40,40);
        } else {
            g.fillOval(drawingWidth/2-20,drawingHeight/2-20,40,40);
        }
    }

}

/*** The following should be in "shapeDialog.java" ***/

import java.awt.*;
import shapeFrame;

class shapeDialog extends Dialog {

    shapeFrame papa;

    shapeDialog(shapeFrame parent) {
        super(parent,"Test",true);
        papa = parent;
        add("North",new Button("Rectangle"));
        add("South",new Button("Oval"));
        pack();
        show();
    }

    public boolean action(Event event,Object what) {
        if (what == "Oval") {
            papa.displayRectangle = false;
            papa.repaint();
            dispose();
            return true;
        }
        if (what == "Rectangle") {
            papa.displayRectangle = true;
            papa.repaint();
            dispose();
            return true;
        }
        return false;
    }

}
```

25

Exercise 17

```
/*** The following should be in "buttons.Java" ***/

import java.awt.*;
import buttonFrame;

class buttons {

    public static void main(String[] param) {
        new buttonFrame();
    }

}

/*** The following should be in "buttonFrame.java" ***/

import java.awt.*;
import buttonDialog;

class buttonFrame extends Frame {

    public buttonFrame() {
        super("Button");
        MenuBar bar = new MenuBar();
        Menu menu = new Menu("File");
        menu.add("Buttons");
        menu.add("Exit");
        bar.add(menu);
        setMenuBar(bar);
        resize(150,100);
        show();
    }

    public boolean handleEvent(Event event) {
        if (event.id == Event.WINDOW_DESTROY) {
            if (event.target == this) {
                return action(event,"Exit");
            }
        }
        return super.handleEvent(event);
    }

    public boolean action(Event event,Object what) {
        if (what == "Exit") {
            System.exit(0);
            return true;
        } else if (what == "Buttons") {
            new buttonDialog(this);
            return true;
        }
        return false;
    }
```

```
    public void paint(Graphics g) {
        g.setColor(Color.red);
        g.fillOval(0,0,40,40);
    }

}

/*** The following should be in "buttonDialog.java" ***/

import java.awt.*;

class buttonDialog extends Dialog {

    buttonDialog(Frame parent) {
        super(parent,"Test",true);
        GridBagConstraints c = new GridBagConstraints();
        GridBagLayout layout = new GridBagLayout();
        Component o;

        setLayout(layout);

        add(o = new Button("A"));
        c.gridx = 0;
        c.gridy = 0;
        c.gridwidth = 2;
        c.gridheight = 1;
        c.fill = GridBagConstraints.BOTH;
        c.weightx = 1;
        c.weighty = 1;
        layout.setConstraints(o,c);

        add(o = new Button("B"));
        c.gridx = 2;
        c.gridy = 0;
        c.gridwidth = 2;
        c.gridheight = 1;
        c.fill = GridBagConstraints.BOTH;
        c.weightx = 1;
        c.weighty = 1;
        layout.setConstraints(o,c);

        add(o = new Button("1"));
        c.gridx = 0;
        c.gridy = 1;
        c.gridwidth = 1;
        c.gridheight = 1;
        c.fill = GridBagConstraints.BOTH;
        c.weightx = 1;
        c.weighty = 1;
        layout.setConstraints(o,c);

        add(o = new Button("2"));
        c.gridx = 1;
        c.gridy = 1;
```

27

continued on next page

continued from previous page

```
            c.gridwidth = 1;
            c.gridheight = 1;
            c.fill = GridBagConstraints.BOTH;
            c.weightx = 1;
            c.weighty = 1;
            layout.setConstraints(o,c);

            add(o = new Button("3"));
            c.gridx = 2;
            c.gridy = 1;
            c.gridwidth = 1;
            c.gridheight = 1;
            c.fill = GridBagConstraints.BOTH;
            c.weightx = 1;
            c.weighty = 1;
            layout.setConstraints(o,c);

            add(o = new Button("4"));
            c.gridx = 3;
            c.gridy = 1;
            c.gridwidth = 1;
            c.gridheight = 1;
            c.fill = GridBagConstraints.BOTH;
            c.weightx = 1;
            c.weighty = 1;
            layout.setConstraints(o,c);

            pack();
            show();
    }

    public boolean action(Event event,Object what) {
        dispose();
        return true;
    }

}
```

Exercise 18

```
/* The following should be in "shape.java" */

import java.awt.*;
import testFrame;
import testDialog;

public class shape {

    public static void main(String[] param) {
        new testFrame();
    }

}
```

```
/* The following should be in "testFrame.java" */

import java.awt.*;
import testDialog;

class testFrame extends Frame {

    boolean shapeIsCircle;
    Color shapeColor;

    public testFrame() {
        super("Dialog test");
        shapeIsCircle = true;
        shapeColor = Color.red;
        MenuBar bar = new MenuBar();
        Menu menu = new Menu("File");
        menu.add("Dialog");
        menu.add("Exit");
        bar.add(menu);
        setMenuBar(bar);
        resize(150,100);
        show();
    }

    public boolean handleEvent(Event event) {
        if (event.id == Event.WINDOW_DESTROY) {
            if (event.target == this) {
                return action(event,"Exit");
            }
        }
        return super.handleEvent(event);
    }

    public boolean action(Event event,Object what) {
        if (what == "Exit") {
            System.exit(0);
            return true;
        } else if (what == "Dialog") {
            new testDialog(this);
            return true;
        }
        return false;
    }

    public void paint(Graphics g) {
        g.setColor(shapeColor);
        if (shapeIsCircle) {
            g.fillOval(0,0,30,30);
        } else {
            g.fillRect(0,0,30,30);
        }
    }

}
```

29

continued on next page

continued from previous page

```java
/* The following should be in "testDialog.java" */

import java.awt.*;
import testFrame;

class testDialog extends Dialog {

    testFrame papa;
    Checkbox circleCheckbox;
    Choice colorChoice;

    testDialog(testFrame parent) {
        super(parent,"Test",true);
        papa = parent;
        CheckboxGroup g;
        Panel p;

        add("South",new Button("OK"));

        p = new Panel();
        p.setLayout(new GridLayout(3,1));
        g = new CheckboxGroup();
        circleCheckbox = new Checkbox("Circle",g,papa.shapeIsCircle);
        p.add(circleCheckbox);
        p.add(new Checkbox("Square",g,!papa.shapeIsCircle));

        colorChoice = new Choice();
        colorChoice.addItem("Green");
        colorChoice.addItem("Red");
        if (papa.shapeColor == Color.green) {
            colorChoice.select(0);
        } else {
            colorChoice.select(1);
        }
        p.add(colorChoice);
        add("Center",p);

        pack();
        show();
    }

    public boolean action(Event event,Object what) {
        if (what == "OK") {
            if (colorChoice.getSelectedIndex() == 0) {
                papa.shapeColor = Color.green;
            } else {
                papa.shapeColor = Color.red;
            }
            papa.shapeIsCircle = circleCheckbox.getState();
            dispose();
            return true;
        }
        return false;
    }

}
```

30

Exercise 19

```
/* This should be in "scroll.java" */

import java.awt.*;
import testFrame;

public class scroll {

    public static void main(String[] s) {
        new testFrame();
    }

}

/* This should be in "testFrame.java" */

import java.awt.*;
import testPanel;

class testFrame extends Frame {

    testPanel panel;

    public testFrame() {
        super("Scroll");
        add("Center",panel = new testPanel());
        resize(100,300);
        show();
    }

    public boolean handleEvent(Event event) {
        if (event.id == Event.WINDOW_DESTROY) {
            if (event.target == this) {
                System.exit(0);
                return true;
            }
        }
        return super.handleEvent(event);
    }

}

/* This should be in "testPanel.java" */

import java.awt.*;

class testPanel extends Panel {

    Scrollbar scrollbar;
    Font font;
    int fontHeight;
    int fontAscent;
    int drawHeight;
```

31

continued on next page

continued from previous page

```
    testPanel() {
        font = null;
        scrollbar = new Scrollbar(Scrollbar.VERTICAL,0,0,0,25);
        setLayout(new BorderLayout());
        add("East",scrollbar);
    }

    public void reshape(int x,int y,int width,int height) {
        super.reshape(x,y,width,height);
        setScrollbar();
    }

    void setScrollbar() {
        if (font == null) {
            return;
        }
        if (size().height < drawHeight) {
            scrollbar.show();
            scrollbar.setValues(0,size().height/fontHeight,0,25);
        } else {
            scrollbar.hide();
            scrollbar.setValue(0);
        }
    }

    public boolean handleEvent(Event event) {
        if (event.target instanceof Scrollbar) {
            repaint();
        }
        return super.handleEvent(event);
    }

    public void paint(Graphics g) {
        int i;
        String alpha = "ABCDEFGHIJKLMNOPQRSTUVWXYZ";
        FontMetrics fontMetrics;

        if (font == null) {
            font = new Font("TimesRoman",Font.PLAIN,24);
            g.setFont(font);
            fontMetrics = g.getFontMetrics();
            fontHeight = fontMetrics.getAscent() + fontMetrics.getDescent()
                + fontMetrics.getLeading();
            fontAscent = fontMetrics.getAscent();
            drawHeight = fontHeight * 26;
            setScrollbar();
        }

        g.setFont(font);
        for (i=scrollbar.getValue(); i<26; ++i) {
            g.drawString(alpha.substring(i,i+1),0,
                (i-scrollbar.getValue())*fontHeight + fontAscent);
        }
    }

}
```

Exercise 20

```
/* The following belongs in "tictac.java". */

import java.awt.*;
import java.applet.Applet;
import Toe;
import positionOccupiedException;

public class tictac extends Applet {

    Toe toe;
    int ticSize;
    boolean turn;
    String msg;
    int winner;

    public final void init() {
        toe = new Toe();
        turn = true;
        msg = "";
        winner = 0;

        if (size().height-50 < size().width) {
            ticSize = (size().height-50)/3;
        } else {
            ticSize = size().width/3;
        }

    }

    public final void paint(Graphics g) {
        int row;
        int col;

        g.drawLine(ticSize,0,ticSize,ticSize*3);
        g.drawLine(ticSize*2,0,ticSize*2,ticSize*3);
        g.drawLine(0,ticSize,ticSize*3,ticSize);
        g.drawLine(0,ticSize*2,ticSize*3,ticSize*2);

        for (row=0; row<3; ++row) {
            for (col=0; col<3; ++col) {
                if (toe.board[row][col] == 1) {
                    g.drawLine(row*ticSize+5,col*ticSize+5,
                        row*ticSize-5+ticSize,col*ticSize-5+ticSize);
                    g.drawLine(row*ticSize-5+ticSize,col*ticSize+5,
                        row*ticSize+5,col*ticSize-5+ticSize);
                } else if (toe.board[row][col] == -1) {
                    g.drawOval(row*ticSize+5,col*ticSize+5,ticSize-10,ticSize-10);
                }
            }
        }
```

continued on next page

continued from previous page

```
        g.drawString(msg,10,3*ticSize+20);
    }

    public boolean mouseDown(Event evt,int x,int y) {
        if (winner != 0) {
            toe.clear();
            winner = 0;
            msg = "";
            repaint();
            return true;
        }
        int row = x/ticSize;
        int col = y/ticSize;
        if ( (row < 3) & (col < 3) ) {
            try {
                toe.set(turn,row,col);
            }
            catch (positionOccupiedException e) {
                msg = "Invalid position";
                repaint();
                return true;
            }
            turn = !turn;
            msg = "";
            winner = toe.winner();
            if (winner == 1) {
                msg = "X wins";
            } else if (winner == -1) {
                msg = "O wins";
            } else if (winner == -2) {
                msg = "No one wins";
            }
            repaint();
        }
        return true;
    }

}

/* The following belongs in "Toe.java" */

import positionOccupiedException;

class Toe {

    int board[][]; // Each position is 0=not occupied, -1=0, 1=X

    /* Constructor */
    Toe() {
        board = new int[3][3];
        clear();
    }

    /* Clear the board */
```

34

```
void clear() {
    int row;
    int col;
    for (row=0; row<3; ++row) {
        for (col=0; col<3; ++col) {
            board[row][col] = 0;
        }
    }
}

/* Set a position on the board */
void set(boolean x,int row,int col) throws positionOccupiedException {
    if (board[row][col] != 0) {
        throw new positionOccupiedException();
    }
    if (x) {
        board[row][col] = 1;
    } else {
        board[row][col] = -1;
    }
}

/* Determine if there is a winner */
/* Return value is -2=no winner, -1=0 wins, 0=no winner yet, 1=X wins */
int winner() {
    int row;
    int col;
    for (row=0; row<3; ++row) {
        if ( (board[row][0] == 1) & (board[row][1] == 1) & (board[row][2] == 1) ) {
            return 1;
        }
        if ( (board[row][0] == -1) & (board[row][1] == -1) & (board[row][2] == -1) )
            return -1;
        }
    }
    for (col=0; col<3; ++col) {
        if ( (board[0][col] == 1) & (board[1][col] == 1) & (board[2][col] == 1) ) {
            return 1;
        }
        if ( (board[0][col] == -1) & (board[1][col] == -1) & (board[2][col] == -1) )
            return -1;
        }
    }
    if ( (board[0][0] == 1) & (board[1][1] == 1) & (board[2][2] == 1) ) {
        return 1;
    }
    if ( (board[2][0] == 1) & (board[1][1] == 1) & (board[0][2] == 1) ) {
        return 1;
    }
    if ( (board[0][0] == -1) & (board[1][1] == -1) & (board[2][2] == -1) ) {
        return -1;
    }
```

35

continued on next page

continued from previous page

```
            if ( (board[2][0] == -1) & (board[1][1] == -1) & (board[0][2] == -1) ) {
                return -1;
            }
            for (row=0; row<3; ++row) {
                for (col=0; col<3; ++col) {
                    if (board[row][col] == 0) {
                        return 0;
                    }
                }
            }
            return -2;
        }

}

/* The following belongs in "positionOccupiedException.java" */

class positionOccupiedException extends Exception {

}
```

Exercise 21

```
/* The following belongs in "test.java" */

import chronos.*;

public class test {

    public static void main(String a[]) {

        date d = new date(2010,5,20);
        time t = new time(11,00);
        datetime dt = new datetime(2007,1,19,13,5);

        d.setYear(2020);
        dt.setYear(2030);

        /* The following would generate an error: */
        /* d.year = 2020; */

    }

}

/* The following belongs in "chronos\date.java" */

package chronos;

public class date {

    private int year;
    private int month;
```

36

```
        private int day;

        public date(int y,int m,int d) {
            setYear(y);
            setMonth(m);
            setDay(d);
        }

        public int getYear() { return year; }
        public int getMonth() { return month; }
        public int getDay() { return day; }

        public void setYear(int y) {
            if (y < 1900) {
                throw new IllegalArgumentException();
            }
            year = y;
        }

        public void setMonth(int m) {
            if ( (m < 1) | (m > 12) ) {
                throw new IllegalArgumentException();
            }
            month = m;
        }

        public void setDay(int d) {
            if ( (d < 1) | (d > 31) ) {
                throw new IllegalArgumentException();
            }
            day = d;
        }

}

/* The following belongs in "chronos\time.java" */

package chronos;

public class time {

    private int hour;
    private int minute;

    public time(int h,int m) {
        setHour(h);
        setMinute(m);
    }

    int getHour() { return hour; }
    int getMinute() { return minute; }

    public void setHour(int h) {
        if ( (h < 0) | (h > 23) ) {
```

37

continued on next page

continued from previous page

```
                throw new IllegalArgumentException();
        }
        hour = h;
    }

    public void setMinute(int m) {
        if ( (m < 0) | (m > 59) ) {
            throw new IllegalArgumentException();
        }
        minute = m;
    }

}

/* The following belongs in "chronos\datetime.java" */

package chronos;

public class datetime {

    private date d;
    private time t;

    public datetime(int y,int m,int day,int h,int m2) {
        d = new date(y,m,day);
        t = new time(h,m2);
    }

    public int getYear() { return d.getYear(); }
    public int getMonth() { return d.getMonth(); }
    public int getDay() { return d.getDay(); }
    public int getHour() { return t.getHour(); }
    public int getMinute() { return t.getMinute(); }

    public void setYear(int y) { d.setYear(y); }
    public void setMonth(int m) { d.setMonth(m); }
    public void setDay(int day) { d.setDay(day); }
    public void setHour(int h) { t.setHour(h); }
    public void setMinute(int m) { t.setMinute(m); }

}
```

38

Exercise 22

```
import java.io.*;

public class atob {

    public static void main(String p[]) {

        DataInputStream inStream;
        try { inStream = new DataInputStream(new BufferedInputStream(
            new FileInputStream("in.txt"))); }
```

```
            catch (Exception e) {
                System.out.println("Unable to open \"in.txt\"");
                return;
            }

            PrintStream outStream;
            try { outStream = new PrintStream(new FileOutputStream("out.txt")); }
            catch (Exception e) {
                System.out.println("Unable to create \"out.txt\"");
                return;
            }

            String line;
            for (;;) {
                try { line = inStream.readLine(); }
                catch (Exception e) {
                    System.out.println("Unable to read from \"in.txt\"");
                    break;
                }
                if (line == null) {
                    break;
                }
                line = line.replace('a','b');
                try { outStream.println(line); }
                catch (Exception e) {
                    System.out.println("Unable to write to \"out.txt\"");
                    System.exit(0);
                }
            }

            try { inStream.close(); }
            catch (Exception e) { ; }
            outStream.close();
        }

}
```

Exercise 23

```
import java.io.*;
import java.net.*;

public class count {

    public static void main(String p[]) {

        URL url;
        try url = new URL("http://...FINISH THE URL HERE...html");
        catch (Exception e) {
            System.out.println("Unable to open HTML file");
            return;
        }
        DataInputStream inStream;
```

continued on next page

continued from previous page

```
            try inStream = new DataInputStream(url.openStream());
            catch (Exception e) {
                System.out.println("Unable to open HTML file");
                return;
            }

            String line;
            int counter = 0;
            int index;
            for (;;) {
                try line = inStream.readLine();
                catch (Exception e) {
                    System.out.println("Unable to read from HTML file");
                    break;
                }
                if (line == null) {
                    break;
                }
                index = line.indexOf('a');
                while (index != -1) {
                    ++counter;
                    index = line.indexOf('a',index+1);
                }
            }

            System.out.println(counter + " a\'s were found in the file.");
            try inStream.close();
            catch (Exception e);
        }

    }
```

PART II

Language Reference

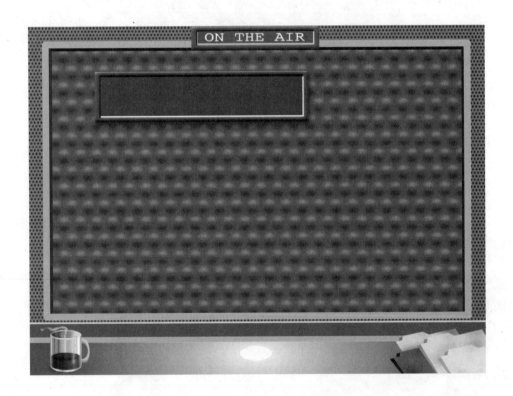

CHAPTER 4

Java™ Language Elements

Line Layout

Java™ code consists of a series of tokens. For example, in the statement

```
total = east + west;
```

the tokens are `total`, `=`, `east`, `+`, `west`, and `;`. You can put any amount of white space *between* tokens. White space includes spaces, tabs, and line breaks. Thus, any of the following are valid representations of the same statement:

```
total = east + west;
total    =    east    +    west;
total =
    east + west;
```

You cannot put spaces *within* a token without changing the meaning of the statement (and possibly making it illegal). For example, the following would be illegal:

```
t   o   tal = east + west;
```

Comments

You can place comments at any point *between* tokens in a Java program. Comments can begin with `/*` and end with `*/`, or they can begin with `//` and end at the end of a line. Comments beginning with `/*` can span several lines. For example, here are some legal comments:

```
total = // this is a one-line comment
    east + /* this is a comment
    that spans several lines */
    west;
```

Names

Various elements of Java can be given names. For example, variables and classes are each given names.

All Java names follow the same rules. A name can consist of letters, digits, underscores (_), and dollar signs ($). A name can have any length. A name cannot begin with a digit.

Names, like most things in Java, are case sensitive. That means the names cat, Cat, and CAT are each unique and identify something different.

Keywords

Many Java statements include keywords. A keyword is simply a word that has a special meaning in Java. For example, in the following statement the word *if* is a keyword:

```
if (a == b) c=d;
```

The important thing to remember about keywords is that you cannot use keywords as names in Java. For example, it is legal to have a variable named *cat*, but not to have a variable named *if*.

The keywords in Java are:

abstract	do	implements	package	throw
boolean	double	import	private	throws
break	else	inner	protected	transient
byte	extends	instanceof	public	try
case	final	int	rest	var
cast	finally	interface	return	void
catch	float	long	short	volatile
char	for	native	static	while
class	future	new	super	
const	generic	null	switch	
continue	goto	operator	synchronized	
default	if	outer	this	

Literals

A literal is something that has a fixed, predefined value. For example, 5 is a literal. There are various kinds of literals in Java, and each follows very specific rules.

Integer Literals

Integer literals are probably the most common kind of literal. Here are some examples:

```
5
-95
22L
0x1f
022
```

An integer literal is normally stored in a Java program as an int value, but you can cause it to be stored as a long by putting either *L* or *l* after it (e.g., 22L). It will also be stored as a long if the value is too large to be stored as a regular int. (You would care whether the literal is stored as a long or an int only in very rare circumstances.)

An integer is normally expressed as a decimal value (e.g., 5) but can also be expressed in hexadecimal (base 16) by preceding it with 0x or 0X (e.g., 0x1f). Following the 0x or 0X can be a sequence of hex digits, and they can be in either upper- or lowercase. For example, 0x1f and 0x1F are both valid integer literals, and they both represent the same value.

An integer can also be expressed as an octal (base 8) value by preceding it with a zero (e.g., 022).

An integer literal can begin with a minus sign (-) to make it a negative number (although, strictly speaking, the minus sign is not part of the literal—it is an operator).

Floating-Point Literals

A floating-point literal represents a floating-point value. Here are some examples:

```
10.2
1e54
-5.34563532e-34
3.4f
```

Most floating-point literals are double literals; that is, they represent a value of type double. If you want the floating-point literal to represent type float, you should follow it with *f* or *F* (e.g., 3.4f).

A floating-point literal can have a base 10 exponent. For example, 1e54 represents 1 times 10 to the 54th power (i.e., 1 followed by 54 zeros). The *e* can be either upper- or lowercase. The exponent can be either positive or negative (e.g., 1e54 or 1e-54).

A floating-point literal always has a decimal point, an exponent, or both. If it had neither, it would be considered an integer literal.

A floating-point literal can begin with a minus sign (-) to make it a negative number (although, strictly speaking, the minus sign is not part of the literal—it is an operator).

Character Literals

A character literal represents a single character. Here are some examples:

```
'a'
'\t'
'\022'
'\u1d5'
```

Character literals always begin and end with a single-quote mark (`'`). Most character literals consist of just one character between those quote marks, although various special forms of characters can be placed there. Those special forms all begin with a backslash character (`\`). Here are the special characters that can be used with a backslash:

```
'\b'  (a backspace character)
'\t'  (a horizontal tab character)
'\n'  (a new line character)
'\r'  (a carriage return character)
'\f'  (a form feed character)
'\"'  (a double-quote character)
'\''  (a single-quote character)
'\\'  (a backslash character)
```

The backslash character can be followed by an octal value, such as `'\022'` to represent the character with an octal value of 22. The largest octal value allowed is `'\0377'`.

The backslash character can be followed by u and then a hex value, such as `'\u1d5'` to represent the character with a hex value of 1d5.

Characters are stored in Java using the Unicode encoding system. That means that each character is represented by 16 bits, so the hex values can be up to `'\uffff'`.

String Literals

A string literal represents an object of the String class. Here are some examples:

```
"The quick brown fox"
"This has\rtwo lines"
"Here are two literals"
    + " combined together"
```

String literals always begin and end with double-quote marks ("). Within the quotes can be any characters (except ") and any of the special values beginning with a backslash that are allowed for character literals.

If you have a very long string literal that doesn't conveniently fit on one line, you can break it into two parts and combine them together with the + concatenation operator.

Operators

Operators mainly perform math, but can also perform a variety of other functions like comparing two values or concatenating two strings.

Most operators fall into one of two categories: binary operators, which work on two operands, and unary operators, which work on one operand. With binary operators, the first operand always appears before the operator, and the second operand appears after it. For example, in a * 3, the *a* and *3* are operands, and the * is an operator. With unary operators, the operator normally appears first. For example, in !*a*, the ! is the operator, and *a* is the operand. (The ++ and −− operators are exceptions to this rule.)

The operators shown in Table 4-1 are the operators provided by Java.

Table 4-1 Operators provided by Java

Operator(s)	Function
+	This operator generally uses two numeric operands. It results in the sum of the operands. If either of the operands is a string, the operator works differently. It converts the non-text operand (if there is one) into text, then concatenates the two strings. The result of the operation is the concatenated string.
-	This operator works only on numeric operands, although it can work on either one or two. If it is used on just one operand, it negates it (converting it from negative to positive or vice versa). If it is used on two operands, it subtracts the second one from the first.
*	This operator works on two numeric operands. It multiplies the first operand by the second.
/	This operator works on two numeric operands. It divides the first operand by the second. If both of the operands are integral (i.e., of type byte, short, int, or long), the result is also integral. In that case, the result is the truncated floating-point result (e.g., 7/4 is 1, not 2).
%	This operator works on two numeric operands. It divides the first operand by the second and results in the remainder of the division (e.g., 5%3 would be 2, because 5/3 is 1 remainder 2).
? :	These two characters combine to form a single operator that uses three operands. The first operand appears before the ?, the second between the ? and the :, and the third following the :. The first operand must be boolean, and the remaining two can be of any type. If the value of the boolean operand is true, the operator returns the value of the second operand; otherwise, it returns the value of the third operand. An example is (a==5) ? 1 : 0, which would have a value of 1 if a is 5, or 0 if not.
!	This operator works on a single boolean operand. It inverts the value of the operand, so true becomes false, and false becomes true.

continued on next page

continued from previous page

Operator(s)	Function
~	This operator works on a single numeric operand. It inverts each of the bits of the operand, so each 1 becomes a 0, and each 0 becomes a 1.
<, >, <=, >=	These operators work on two numeric operands. They compare the value of the first operand to the second and return a boolean that indicates how the two compare. The < operator will be true if the first operand is less than the second; > will be true if the first operand is greater than the second; <= will be true if the first operand is less than or equal to the second; and >= will be true if the first operand is greater than or equal to the second.
!=, ==	These operators work in two different situations. In the first situation, both operands are numeric. In that case, == will be true if the operands have the same numeric value, and != will be true if the operands do not have the same numeric value. In the second situation, the two operands for these operators are objects. (Null can be used in place of one of the objects.) In that case, == will be true if the two operands are the same object, and != will be true if the two operands are not the same object.
&	This operator works on either two integer values or on two boolean values. If used with two integer values, it will return the two integers and ed together (i.e., each bit will be 1 only if the corresponding bit in both of the operands is 1). If this operator is used with two boolean values, it will return true if both of the operands are true. (See the discussion later in the chapter, entitled "Comparing & with &&.")
|	This operator works on either two integer values or on two boolean values. If used with two integer values, it will return the two integers ored together (i.e., each bit will be 1 if either of the corresponding bits in the operands is 1). If this operator is used with two boolean values, it will return true if either of the operands is true. (See the discussion below, entitled "Comparing & with &&.")
^	This operator works on either two integer values or on two boolean values. If used with two integer values, it will return the two integers exclusively ored together (i.e., each bit will be 1 if either of the corresponding bits in the operands is 1, but not if both of the corresponding bits are 1). If this operator is used with two boolean values, it will return true if either of the operands is true, but not if both of the operands are true.

48

Operator(s)	Function
&&	This operator works on two boolean operands. It will return true if both of the operands are true. (See the discussion below, entitled "Comparing & with &&.")
||	This operator works on two boolean operands. It will return true if either of the operands is true. (See the discussion below, entitled "Comparing & with &&.")
++	This operator works on just one operand, and that operand can appear either before or after the ++. It adds 1 to the operand, storing that new value in the operand. The value returned by the ++ (i.e., the value used in the surrounding expression) will depend on whether ++ is placed before or after the operand. It will return the value of the operand before the addition if the operator is placed before the operand, or the value of the operand after the addition if the operator is placed after the operand. For example, in the statement a = (b++), the value assigned to a will be the value of b after adding 1 to it, since the ++ appears after the b. In the statement a = (++b), the value assigned to a will be the value of b before adding 1 to it.
- -	This operator works on just one operand, and that operand can appear either before or after the --. It subtracts 1 from the operand, storing that new value in the operand. The value returned by the -- (i.e., the value used in the surrounding expression) will depend on whether -- is placed before or after the operand. It will be the value of the operand before the subtraction if the operator is placed before the operand, or the value of the operand after the subtraction if the operator is placed after the operand. For example, in the statement a = (b--) the value assigned to a will be the value of b after subtracting 1 from it, since the -- appears after the b. In the statement a = (--b), the value assigned to a will be the value of b before subtracting 1 from it.
<<	This operator shifts the bits in the first operand to the left by the number of positions specified by the second operand. For example, a<<3 would shift the bits in a left by 3 positions. The bits shifted off the left-hand end of the value are lost. Zero bits will be shifted onto the right-hand end.
>>	This operator shifts the bits in the first operand to the right by the number of positions specified by the second operand. For example, a>>3 would shift the bits in a right by 3 positions.

49

continued on next page

continued from previous page

Operator(s)	Function
	The bits shifted off the right-hand end of the value are lost. The high-order (leftmost) bit will be duplicated to create new bits on the left-hand end. (This form is appropriate for signed values, while >>> is more appropriate for unsigned values.)
>>>	This operator shifts the bits in the first operand to the right by the number of positions specified by the second operand. For example, a>>>3 would shift the bits in a right by 3 positions. The bits shifted off the right-hand end of the value are lost. Zero bits will be shifted onto the left-hand end. (This form is appropriate for unsigned values, while >> is more appropriate for signed values.)
=	This operator assigns the value of the second operand to the first operand.
*=, /=, -=, +=, %=	These operators perform the given numeric calculation on the first operand. For example, a += 3 would add 3 to a.
&=, |=, ^=	These operators perform the given logical operation on the first operand. For example, a &= 3 will calculate the value a & 3 and store it in a.
<<=, >>=, >>>=	These operators perform the given shift operation on the first operand. For example a << 3 would shift a left by 3 bits and store the result in a.
instanceof	This operator uses an object as the first operand and a class name (or interface name) as the second operand. It will return true if the object belongs to the class (or it implements the interface).

50

Comparing & with &&

The **&** and **&&** operators perform similar functions when used on boolean operators. (The same is true of | and ||.) The only difference between **&** and **&&** is how much of the expression is evaluated. For example, look at these two expressions:

```
(a == 5) & ((b++) > 3)
(a == 5) && ((b++) > 3)
```

Suppose that *a* is not equal to 5. In that case, the Java interpreter doesn't need to evaluate ((b++) > 3) since it knows the entire expression must be false. But perhaps it should evaluate the ((b++) > 3) anyway, since there might be some effect of doing that evaluation. (In this case there is such an effect: *b* will be increased by 1.) How does the interpreter decide whether to be efficient by skipping the `((b++) > 3)`, or thorough by evaluating it? It knows by which operator you use. The **&** operator will cause the entire expression to be evaluated, while the **&&** operator allows Java to skip evaluating parts it doesn't need to.

The same rule applies to **|** and **||**.

Expressions

Expressions are built by combining together operators, operands, and parentheses. For example, here are some valid Java expressions:

```
5
a
5 + a
(5+a) * 3
```

The order in which an expression is evaluated by Java can affect the value of the expression. For example, consider the following expression:

```
5 + 3 * 2
```

The value of that expression will be 16 if the addition is performed first, or 11 if the multiplication is performed first. To avoid any doubt, you can tell Java which operation to perform by adding parentheses, as in these examples:

```
(5 + 3) * 2
5 + (3 * 2)
```

51

The first version will perform the addition first, and the second will perform the multiplication first.

If you choose not to add parentheses to an expression, Java will evaluate certain operators before others. For example, multiplication is always done before addition. That is because multiplication has a higher precedence than addition. Here is a list of the Java operators, in order of precedence (the high-precedence operators are first):

```
++ -- + - ~ ! casting
* / %
+ -
<< >> >>>
< <= > >= instanceof
== !=
&
^
|
&&
||
?:
= *= /= += -= <<= >>= >>>= &= ^= |=
```

The + and − on the first row of the list are the unary versions of the operators. The + and − on the third row are the binary versions. Operators on the same row have the same precedence and will be evaluated in the order they appear in the expression (left to right).

Integer Data Types

There are four types of integers in Java: byte, short, int, and long. They can all be used to store both positive and negative integer values. The only difference among them is the amount of storage they take and the range of integers they provide. Those values are shown in Table 4-2.

Table 4-2 Integer data types

Type	Space	Range
byte	1 byte	-128 to 127
short	2 bytes	-32,768 to 32,767
int	4 bytes	-2,147,483,648 to 2,147,483,647
long	8 bytes	-9,223,372,036,854,775,808 to 9,223,372,036,854,775,807

In choosing an integer type, keep in mind that all the numeric operators (+, *, etc.) return a type of long if one of the operands is long, or int if not. This means that using short or byte variables can require you to perform extra casting. For example:

```
int a;
a = 5 * 27;

short b;
b = (short)(5 * 27);
```

The first two lines of code don't require a cast, because the result of 5 * 27 is an int. The second two lines of code need a cast to convert to a short.

Floating-Point Data Types

There are two types of floating-point values in Java: float and double. They can both be used to store floating-point values. They differ in the amount of storage used to hold the values. This results in a higher precision for double than float, as well as a wider range of values, as shown below in Table 4-3.

Table 4-3 Floating-point data types

Type	Space	Approximate Range
float	4 bytes	-3e38 to 3e38
double	8 bytes	-1e308 to 1e308

In choosing a floating-point type, keep in mind that all the numeric operators (**+**, *****, etc.) return a type of double. That means that using float variables can require you to perform extra casting. For example:

```
double a;
a = 5.2 * 3.9;

float b;
b = (float)(5.2 * 3.9);
```

The first two lines of code don't require a cast, because the result of **5.2 * 3.9** is a double. The second two lines of code need a cast to convert that double into a float.

Boolean Data Type

The boolean type can hold only two values: true and false.

Character Data Types

There are two data types that hold characters: **char** and **String**. (Strictly speaking, **String** is a class, not a native Java data type. It will be treated as a native data type in this discussion because it acts more like a native data type than a class.)

The key difference between these two types is that a **char** variable can hold only one character, while a **String** can hold any number of characters.

The characters are stored using the Unicode encoding scheme, which means that each character uses 16 bits (2 bytes) of storage.

In using **char** and **String** variables, it is important to keep in mind the difference between character and string literals. For example, look at this code:

```
char c = 'a'; // legal
char d = "a"; // illegal – char can't use a string literal
String s = 'a';// illegal – string can't use a char literal
String t = "a";// legal
```

Casting

Casting is a process used to convert from one type of data to another. It involves putting the type you want to convert to inside parentheses, as in this example which converts a long into a short:

```
long a=5;
short b;
b = (short)a;
```

Casting can be used to perform any of the following kinds of conversions:

- Convert from one numeric data type to another. This can be done with any of the native data types: byte, short, int, long, float, and double.
- Convert from char to a numeric data type, or from a numeric data type to `char`.
- Convert from one object type to another. This requires that the source object type be a subclass of the destination object type.

```
long a = 5;
```

When converting from one numeric data type to another, casting is required only if the conversion might lose information. For example, you can convert from a short to a long without a cast, because no information could be lost in the process. But, to convert from a long to a short, you must supply a cast, because information might be lost in the process. (Adding a cast to a statement is a way of telling Java you understand that data might be lost.) Here are some examples:

```
short s = 4;
a = s;            // cast not required
a = (long)s;      // cast allowed, but not required
s = (short)a;     // cast required
```

Arrays

An array is a series of items, each of which is identified by its location in the series. This location is called an index or subscript. The items in an array can be either native Java data types or objects. Here is an example of creating an array of int and an array of `Date` objects:

```
int i[]; // You can also use "int[] i;"
Date d[]; // You can also use "Date[] d;"
i = new int[10];
d = new Date[10];
```

Each array in the above examples has 10 elements. To use one of those 10 elements, you must specify which one you want with an index. The index is a numeric expression contained in brackets, as in the following examples:

```
i[5] = 12;  // puts "12" in the 6th element of array "i"
d[0].setMonth(9);  // calls "setMonth(9)" for the 1st element of array "d"
```

The index for an array should have a value of zero to use the first element, one to use the second element, and so on. Any numeric expression can be used in the brackets, as shown in the following example:

```
int a = 5;
i[a+2] = 29; // References the 8th element of array "i"
```

Arrays that use just one index are called one-dimensional arrays. You can have arrays of any number of dimensions. Here is an example of a two-dimensional array:

```
int t[][];
t = new int[10][5];
```

You can think of a one-dimensional array as a list of values. You can think of a two-dimensional array as a table of values, placed in rows and columns. Here are some examples:

```
t[0][0] = 5;  // Stores a value in the first column of the first row
t[1][0] = 22; // Stores a value in the first column of the second row
t[5][2] = 60; // Stores a value in the third column of the sixth row
```

You can use an array reference any place that a simple variable would be allowed. For example, notice where the simple int variable *q* is used in this statement:

```
r = 5 + q*3;
```

Because that statement is valid for a simple int, it is also valid for an element of an int array, as in this example:

```
r = 5 + i[2]*3;
```

Array variables are objects, and they have one field variable: length. That variable contains the number of elements in the array. Here is an example of using it:

```
int i;
int a[] = new int[10];
for (i=0; i<a.length; ++i) {
    a[i] = -1;
        }
```

55

CHAPTER 5

Java™ Program Structure

The Big Picture

There are two types of Java™ programs: applications and applets. Applets are small pieces of code that are included in a Web page. They are run automatically by the Web browser when the page is displayed. An application, on the other hand, is much more like a traditional program. It is run by the user entering a command to the system. The command instructs the Java interpreter to begin executing the application.

The internal structure of both applications and applets is similar. The only difference is that an applet includes a subclass of the Applet class, while an application includes a class with a *main* method. For an applet, the Applet subclass contains the methods the Web browser will call (such as *paint*). For an application, the *main* method is the method the Java interpreter will call to start the application.

Programs, whether applets or applications, are made up of a collection of "packages." Packages, in turn, consist of a series of source files. Each source file contains a collection of classes. Figure 5-1 shows the relationship of these items.

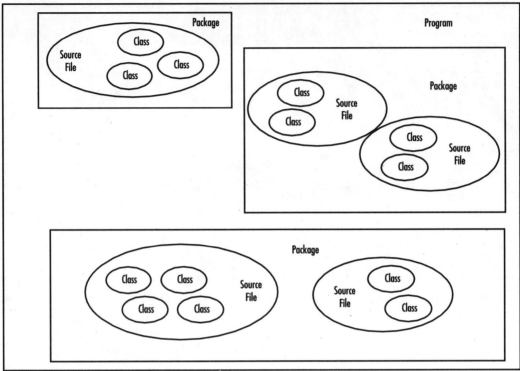

Figure 5-1 Program structure

Packages

Every source file in a Java program is part of a package. A source file can begin with a package statement, which indicates what package the source file belongs to. Here is an example of a package statement for a source file in the Chronos package:

```
package Chronos;
```

If a source file doesn't begin with a package statement, the file is assumed to be part of the default, unnamed package.

Packages are a convenient way of grouping together source files. All the source files in a package should reside in the same directory. The name of that directory can be partially specified by the name of the package. For example, suppose the following statement appears in a Java program:

```
import misc.Chronos.*;
```

This will cause the Java compiler to look for a package named Chronos. It will search all the directories in the CLASSPATH environment variable, plus the current directory, for a directory named misc. If it finds a directory by that name, it will search that directory for a directory named Chronos. If it finds Chronos, it will assume that all the source files in it are part of the misc.Chronos package.

The classes in a given package have greater access to other classes in the same package than they do to classes in other packages. (For more information about this, see the section below entitled "Access Control.")

Source Files

Each Java source file can begin with a package statement. Following that statement, if any, can be some import statements. The remainder of the source file consists of class definitions. Any number of classes can be defined in a Java source file. The only restriction is that only one of the classes in the file can be declared public. Further, if a class is declared public, the name of that class must exactly match the name of the source file (except for the .java extension). For example, only a source file named date.java can contain this class definition:

```
public class date {
    /* ... */
}
```

In place of a series of class definitions, a source file can contain a single interface definition. In that case, the name of the interface must exactly match the name of the source file (except for the .java extension).

Class Headers

Each class is defined in just one place. That definition begins with a class header, like this:

```
public class date
```

Following the class header are a pair of braces, which contain the class definition.

The header can optionally include the keywords shown below before the class keyword; see Table 5-1.

Table 5-1 Keywords that may appear in class headers

Keyword	Function
public	This keyword indicates that the class can be used by any other class. For more details, see the section entitled "Access Control," below.

continued on next page

continued from previous page

Keyword	Function
abstract	This means the class is an abstract class. You cannot create objects of an abstract class, but if it has a subclass (which isn't abstract), you can create objects of that subclass. An abstract class usually includes one or more abstract methods. (An abstract method is one which doesn't have a method body. The abstract methods must be overridden in a subclass to provide the method bodies.)
final	This means the class cannot have subclasses.

Following the class name, the class header can optionally have an extends clause. That clause specifies the class that is the superclass of the one being defined. Here is an example of such a header, which makes car a subclass of vehicle:

```
public class car extends vehicle
```

Following the extends clause, if any, can optionally be an implements clause. Here is an example of a class header with an implements clause:

```
public class circle extends Applet implements Runnable
```

In this example, the class implements the Runnable interface. (That means the class must supply all the methods defined in the Runnable interface.) Several interface names can be included in an implements clause, separated by commas.

Fields

Following a class header are a pair of braces. Within those braces can be any number of field definitions and static initializers. There are two types of fields: field variables and field methods. The fields and static initializers can be defined in any order.

Here is an example of a class that includes four field variables (year, month, day, and highestYear), one method definition (set), and one static initializer (highestYear = 1900):

```
public class date {
    int year;
    int month;
    int day;
    static int highestYear;
    {
        highestYear = 1900;
    }
    void set(int year,int month,int day) {
        this.year = year;
        this.month = month;
        this.day = day;
    }
}
```

The definitions of field variables follow the rules for variable declaration statements. (See "Variable Declaration Statements" in Chapter 6, "Statements.")

The definitions of methods follow the rules described in the next section, "Methods."

Static initializers are simply a series of Java statements inside braces. Those statements will be executed once, the first time an object of that class is used. The code is generally used to initialize any static variables the class may have, although it can be used for any one-time initialization related to the class.

Methods

Each method begins with a method header. For example, here is a typical header:

```
long sum(int count)
```

This header identifies a method which returns a *long* value, is named sum, and takes a single *int* parameter (named count).

Preceding the return type in a method header can be any of the Java keywords shown in Table 5-2.

Table 5-2 Java keywords that may appear in a method header

Keyword	Function
public	This indicates that the method can be used by any other method. (For more information, see the "Access Control" section below.)
private	This indicates that the method can only be used by other methods in the same class. (For more information, see "Access Control," below.)
protected	This indicates that the method can only be used by other methods in the same class or by methods in a subclass of this class. (For more information, see "Access Control," below.)
static	Generally, a method operates on an object of its class. For example, start.set(1900,10,10) might call method *set* for object *start*. If the keyword *static* is used on a method header, that means the method doesn't operate on individual objects. Instead, it operates on the class as a whole and would be called with the class name. For example, date.count() might be a call to a *static* method named *count* for a class named *date*. (Note that the method body cannot reference field variables of the class as if they were local variables. That's because there is no object associated with the call to the method, so no field variables are directly available.)

61

continued on next page

continued from previous page

Keyword	Function
abstract	This indicates that the method is abstract. That means the body for the method is not supplied as part of this class. The body must be supplied by a subclass.
final	This indicates that the method cannot be overridden by a subclass.
native	This indicates that the method is not provided in Java. Instead, it is written in a different language and supplied in a library.
synchronized	This indicates that the method can only run if no other methods which are identified as *synchronized* are running on the same object at the same time. If another such method is already running when this method is called, the call will be delayed until the other method is finished.

Following the list of keywords in the method header comes the method return type. This can be any of the native Java types (int, float, etc.) or any object type. It can also be void if the method returns nothing.

Following the method's return type is the method name, then an open parenthesis, then the list of parameters and then a close parenthesis. (The parentheses must be supplied even if there are no parameters.) There can be any number of parameters, and they should be separated from one another with commas. The parameters follow the same rules as variable declarations except that they cannot be followed by an initializer.

The last thing in a method header can be a throws clause. It lists all the exceptions that are thrown by the method. This clause is required if the method throws any exceptions that are not RuntimeExceptions. It consists of the word throws followed by a list of exception names, separated by commas. (For more information about exceptions, see "Exception Handling Statements" in Chapter 6.)

Following the method header is a pair of braces. Inside the braces is the method body—the code which is executed when the method is called. It can include any of the statements described in Chapter 6. If the method is declared *abstract*, the braces and the method body are replaced by a semicolon.

Method Overloading

Several methods in a class can be given the same name. This is called overloading the method. When looking at a method call, the Java compiler determines which method is being called by examining the parameter list.

For example, here are two overloaded methods:

```
void set(int year) {
    /* ... */
}
void set(int year,int month,int day) {
    /* ... */
}
```

If you use a call like the following, it is clear you are calling the second version of set since there are three parameters:

```
a.set(2010,5,1);
```

Similarly, the following is clearly calling the first version of set:

```
a.set(2010);
```

To be overloaded, two methods must have parameter lists which are different enough to allow Java to tell which method is being called. For example, these method definitions would be illegal because the parameter lists have the same number and type of parameters:

```
void set(int year) {
    /* ... */
}
void set(int month) {
    /* ... */
}
```

The following methods would also be illegal, since they differ only by the return type:

```
int set(int year) {
    /* ... */
}
void set(int month) {
    /* ... */
}
```

These would be legal, since they have different parameter lists (even though they have the same number of parameters):

```
void set(String s) {
    /* ... */
}
void set(int year) {
    /* ... */
}
```

Constructors

Classes can include a special kind of method called a constructor. A constructor is called when an object is created. For example, suppose you have a class like this:

```
public class date {
    int year;
    int month;
    int day;
    date(int year) {
        this.year = year;
        month = 1;
        day = 1;
    }
}
```

The method named *date* is a constructor. Constructors have two unique characteristics. First, a constructor's name always exactly matches the name for the class. Second, constructors do not have a return type (not even void).

To create an object of the above class, you must supply the parameter to the constructor. For example, this would do it:

```
date d = new date(2010);
```

The *new* operator will reserve space for the date object and will then call the constructor. The constructor is responsible for performing any initialization necessary for the object. The fact that the constructor is called automatically when an object is created means that an object cannot be created without being properly initialized.

Constructors can be overloaded just as regular methods can. Here is an example of a class with an overloaded constructor:

```
public class date {
    int year;
    int month;
    int day;
    date(int year) {
        this.year = year;
        month = 1;
        day = 1;
    }
    date(int year,int month,int day) {
        this.year = year;
        this.month = month;
        this.day = day;
    }
}
```

You could create an object of that class with statements like either of the following:

```
date a = new date(2010);
date b = new date(2010,5,15);
```

Naturally, the first statement will call the first constructor, because it has just one parameter. The second statement has three parameters, so it will call the second constructor.

If a class has at least one constructor, then a constructor will always be called when an object is created. This means you must always supply the appropriate parameters for at least one of the constructors.

The same rule applies to constructors of a superclass. If a class has a superclass and that superclass has at least one constructor, then a constructor of the superclass must be called when an object is created. It is generally the responsibility of the subclass constructor to make a call to a superclass constructor. If the subclass constructor doesn't call the superclass constructor and the superclass has a constructor with no parameters, Java will call that superclass constructor automatically. But, if all the superclass constructors require parameters, Java won't be able to call one of them—in that case, the subclass constructor is required to make a call.

Here is an example:

```
class animal {
    animal() {
        /* ... */
    }
}
class cat extends animal {
    cat() {
        super();
        /* ... */
    }
}
```

In this example, the subclass constructor is calling the superclass constructor. (Notice how it uses the keyword *super* to do that.) In this case, the call to *super* isn't required. Since the superclass constructor has no parameters, Java will call the superclass constructor if the subclass constructor doesn't.

Here is another example:

```
class animal {
    animal(int age) {
        /* ... */
    }
}
class cat extends animal {
    cat() {
        super(5);
        /* ... */
    }
}
```

In this example, there are no superclass constructors without parameters. That means the subclass constructor is *required* to call the superclass constructor.

When a subclass constructor calls a superclass constructor, it must be done at the very beginning of the subclass constructor. No other processing can be done first.

Calling Methods

Suppose you have a method defined as follows:

```
public class date {
    void set(int year) {
        /* ... */
    }
}
```

Before you can call the method, you must have a date object. You can create one like this:

```
date d = new date();
```

You can then use the object to call the method like this:

```
d.set(2010);
```

Notice how the call to the method begins with *d*. That identifies *d* as the object that will be processed by the method.

In the example above, the method had a return type of void. That means that there is only one way to call the method: with a call statement. This is a statement which consists solely of a call to a method.

If a method has a return type other than void, you can also call the method from within an expression. For example, suppose the method is defined like this:

```
public class date {
    int set(int year) {
        /* ... */
    }
}
```

That would let you use a call to the method (for object *d*) in an expression, like this:

```
if (d.set(2010) > 12) {
    /* ... */
}
```

Because the method returns an int, you can use a call to the method any place an int value can be used.

The examples shown above are for methods which are not static. The rules for calling a static method are similar. Just like a non-static method, you can always call a static method from a call statement. You can also call the method from within an expression if the method returns a value. The only difference is that you don't use an object to call a static method. Instead, you use the class name. Here is an example:

```
public class date {
    static void set(int year) {
        /* ... */
    }
}
```

You might call that method with a statement like this:

```
date.set(2010);
```

Interfaces

A Java source file generally contains one or more classes. Instead, it can contain an interface. For example, here is an interface which is commonly used in applets:

```
public interface Runnable {
    public void run();
}
```

An interface defines a series of abstract methods, such as *run* in the example above. Any class which claims to implement that interface (i.e., which includes that interface in the implements clause in its class header) must supply all those abstract methods.

An interface begins with an interface header. That header normally begins with public, but does not have to. Supplying public means that any class can use the interface. Not supplying public means the interface can only be used by classes in the same package.

Following the word public, if supplied, is the word interface followed by the name of the interface. That constitutes the interface header. Following the header are a pair of braces which enclose the body of the interface.

The body consists of a series of method definitions. They have the same form as abstract methods in a class: They have a semicolon in place of the body of the method. The only difference between the way an abstract method is defined in a class and the way a method is defined in an interface is that the word *abstract* is optional in an interface.

Access Control

Many times, you want to limit access to certain portions of a class. For example, if you have a field variable that contains a year, you might want to ensure that the year is always stored with a century (i.e., as 2010, not 10). You can help ensure that by limiting the parts of a program that have access to the field variable to a few trusted methods. The access control feature of Java lets you do that.

There are three kinds of items in Java which can have limited access: classes, interfaces, and fields (both field variables and field methods).

Access to interfaces is very simple. If the interface header includes the word public, the interface can be used by any part of a program. If it lacks public, it can only be used by classes in the same package as the interface.

Access to classes is similar to that for interfaces. If the class header includes the word public, the class can be used by any part of a program. If it lacks public, it can only be used by classes in the same package. Only one class in each source file is allowed to be public.

Access to fields is a bit more complicated. Each field, whether a field variable or a field method, can include any of the following four phrases: public, protected, private protected, or private. In addition to using one of those four phrases, a field can also use none of them, which provides a fifth level of access. The access for each of these five levels is shown in Table 5-3.

Table 5-3 Field access levels

Keyword	Access
public	Access is allowed by any part of the program.
none	Access is allowed only by classes in the same package.
protected	Access is allowed by classes in the same package, and by classes which are subclasses of the protected class.
private protected	Access is allowed by methods in the same class or subclasses of the private protected class.
private	Access is allowed only by methods in the private class.

CHAPTER 6

Statements

Variable Declaration Statements

One of the most common kinds of statements in Java™ is the variable declaration statement. You can use it to declare variables of any of the native Java types (such as int or double), or any object type.

The simplest form of declaration statement looks like this:

```
int a;
date b;
```

The first example declares a single integer variable *a*, and the second declares a date object variable, *b*. These statements illustrate that a variable declaration statement always begins with a keyword that indicates a native Java type (such as int), or the name of a class (such as date).

If you wish, you can declare several variables in one statement, as in these examples:

```
int a,b;
date c,d;
```

If you wish, you can assign a value to a variable, as in this example:

```
int a=5,b;
```

Notice that when you initialize a variable, it only affects that single variable (*a* in this case). The others (such as *b*) can be initialized separately, or they can remain uninitialized.

If you wish, you can declare arrays, as in these examples:

```
int a[],b;
int[] c,d;
date e[],f;
date[] g,h;
```

If you put the brackets after the name of a variable, only that variable will be an array—the others in the same statement are not affected. If you put the brackets after the data type, all the variables in the statement will be arrays. Thus, *b* is not an array, but *a, c,* and *d* are arrays.

Arrays can be initialized by putting the values inside braces, as in the following example:

```
int a[] = {22,33,44};
```

That statement would be identical to the following code:

```
int a[];
a = new int[3];
a[0] = 22;
a[1] = 33;
a[2] = 44;
```

The type (such as int or date) can be preceded by any of several keywords. Those keywords are allowed only if the variable declaration is for a field variable, not a local variable or parameter. The keywords are shown in Table 6-1.

Table 6-1 Available keywords

Keyword	Function
public	This keyword means that any method may use or change the variable. (For more information, see "Access Control" in Chapter 5, "Java™ Program Structure.")
protected	This keyword means the variable may be used only by methods in the same package or methods which are sub-classes of the current class. (For more information, see "Access Control" in Chapter 5.)
private	This keyword means the variable may only be used by methods in the class to which the field variable belongs. (For more information, see "Access Control" in Chapter 5.)
static	This keyword means the variable exists just once, not once for each object in the class. You reference a static variable by preceding it with the class name (rather than an object name). For example, date.highestYear=2010 would assign a value to static field variable highestYear of class date.
final	This keyword means the variable isn't really a variable at all, but a constant. It must be initialized in the variable declaration statement, and it will always retain that constant value.
volatile	This keyword means the variable may be modified by other threads or tasks. As a result, the Java compiler will always read its value from permanent memory when it is used, rather than relying on a copy that might be hanging around in a register or other temporary location.

Expression Statements

The term expression statement is a bit of a misnomer, since you can't make a statement of just any old expression. For example, the following would all be illegal:

```
a;
5;
1-b*5+3;
```

There are, however, a few special forms of expressions that are valid statements.

One example is a call to a method. Most commonly, they consist of an object name, followed by a period, followed by the name of the method being called, as in the following example which calls the set method:

```
date d = new date();
d.set(2010,5,10);
```

For more information about calling methods, see "Calling Methods" in Chapter 5.

Expressions that increment and decrement a variable can be statements. They simply consist of a variable name either preceded or followed by the increment operator (++) or the decrement operator (--). Here are some examples:

```
++a;
total++;
--c;
```

Expressions which allocate storage space with the *new* operator can be statements. Most commonly, a new object is created with an assignment statement, as in this example:

```
date d;
d = new date();
```

There are some situations, however, when you don't need to save a reference to the new object. In that case, you don't need to use an assignment statement; instead, you can use an expression statement, like this:

```
new date();
```

Assignment Statements

One of the most basic statements in Java is the assignment statement. It assigns a new value to a variable. The most common form uses the equal (=) operator, as in this example:

```
a = 5;
```

In addition to the equal operator (=), assignment statements can use any of the variations of that operator, such as plus-equal (+=) or shift-equal (>>=). Some examples are:

```
total += salary;
flag >>= 3;
```

For more information about the various equal operators, see "Operators" in Chapter 4, "Java™ Language Elements."

if Statements

An *if* statement commonly looks like the following example:

```
if (a == 5) {
    /* ... */
}
```

In this example, the statements between the braces will be executed only *if* the condition is true, which in this case means that *a* has a value of 5. An *if* statement always begins with the keyword *if*, and is followed by an expression in parentheses. That expression must have a boolean value. Following the expression will normally be a series of statements inside braces. You can substitute a single statement, as in the following example, if you wish:

```
if (a == 5) /* statement here */;
```

An *if* statement can be immediately followed by an *else* statement. The body of the *else* will be executed only if the condition in the *if* is false. Here is an example:

```
if (a == 5) {
    /* statements executed if expression is true */
} else {
    /* statements executed if expression is false */
}
```

Like an *if* statement, the *else* statement can use a single statement, rather than a series of statements inside braces. Here is an example:

```
if (a == 5) {
    /* statements executed if expression is true */
}
else /* statement executed if expression is false */;
```

switch Statements

The *switch* statement lets you select one of several bits of code to be executed. The selection is based on the value of an expression. Here is an example:

```
switch (a+5) {
    case 1:
        /* statements here */
        break;
    case 2:
        /* statements here */
        break;
    default:
        /* statements here */
        break;
}
```

If a+5 has a value of 1, the statements following case 1 will be executed. If a+5 has a value of 2, the statements following case 2 will be executed. If a+5 has any other value, the statements following default will be executed.

You can have as many different cases in a *switch* statement as you wish, although each must have a unique value. You can have only one default label, although you can omit it if you wish. If there is no default label and the expression doesn't match any of the *case* labels, then none of the code is executed.

The expression in the *switch* statement must be of type char, byte, short, or int. The values following case must be literals (not expressions), and must be of type char, byte, short, or int.

When a *break* statement is encountered, the execution of the *switch* statement ends. A common mistake is to forget the *break* statement, which can cause code to be executed that you didn't expect to be executed. In the following example, the statement b=5 will be executed whether *a* is 1 or 2:

```
switch (a) {
    case 1:
        b=4;
    case 2:
        b=5;
}
```

Because the execution of a *switch* statement can continue from one case to another, you are allowed to have several *case* values for one piece of code, as in this example:

```
switch (a) {
    case 1:
    case 2:
    case 3:
        b = true;
        break;
    default:
        b = false;
        break;
}
```

while and *do* Statements

The *while* and *do* statements allow you to cause a piece of code to be executed over and over. Here is an example:

```
while (sum < 100) {
    sum += 10;
    i++;
}
```

This code will cause the two statements inside the braces to be executed repeatedly, until *sum* reaches 100.

A *while* statement always begins with the keyword *while*, which is followed by an expression in parentheses. The expression must have a boolean value. Normally a series of statements inside braces follows the expression, although a single statement (without braces) can be substituted as in this example:

```
while (sum < 100)
    sum += 10;
```

A *do* statement looks very similar to a *while*:

```
do {
    sum += 10;
    i++;
} while (sum < 100);
```

In fact, the example above performs almost exactly the same processing as:

```
while (sum < 100) {
    sum += 10;
    i++;
}
```

The only difference between the two examples is that the *do* statement will always execute the loop at least once, whereas the *while* statement won't execute the loop even once if the condition is initially false. That is because a *while* statement checks the condition at the beginning of each loop (as its placement before the loop suggests), but the *do* statement checks the condition at the end of each loop (as its placement suggests).

74

for Statements

The *for* statement uses syntax that is a bit tricky to get used to, but it can be a very powerful statement. Like the *do* and *while* statements, the *for* statement causes some code to be executed repeatedly, in a loop. Here is an example:

```
for (i=0; i<10; ++i) {
    total += a[i];
}
```

As you can see, the *for* statement consists of the word *for* followed by a pair of parentheses. Inside the parentheses are three clauses, separated by semicolons. The first clause is an expression statement, and is executed only once—before the first time through the loop. The second clause is an expression which must have a boolean value. As long as this condition remains true, the loop will continue executing. The third clause is another expression statement, and it will be executed at the end of each loop.

A *for* statement is similar to a *while* statement. In fact, a *for* statement can always be rewritten as a *while*. Here is a *while* which performs exactly the same processing as the earlier *for* statement:

```
i=0;
while (i<10) {
    total += a[i];
    ++i;
}
```

The parentheses in a *for* statement are normally followed by a pair of braces enclosing several statements. They can, instead, be followed by a single statement, as in this example:

```
for (i=0; i<10; ++i)
    total += a[i];
```

The first and third clauses of the *for* statement can be replaced by a series of expression statements, separated by commas, as in this example:

```
for (i=0,j=0; i<10; ++i,j+=2) {
    total += a[i] + b[j];
}
```

The first clause of a *for* statement can be replaced by a variable declaration statement, as in this example, which declares the *int* variable i:

```
for (int i=0; i<10; ++i) {
    total += a[i];
}
```

break and *continue* Statements

The *break* and *continue* statements are used in *for*, *do*, and *while* loops. (The *break* statement can also be used in *switch* statements; for information about this, see the "*switch* Statements" section, above.)

The *break* statement causes the execution of the loop to end. For example:

```
for (i=0; i<10; ++i) {
    if (a[i] = -1) {
        break;
    }
    total += a[i];
}
```

In this case, if the value a[i] is found to be -1, the execution of the *for* loop will end.

The *continue* statement causes the loop to continue, but terminates the current iteration through the loop. For example:

```
for (i=0; i<10; ++i) {
    if (a[i] = -1) {
        continue;
    }
    total += a[i];
}
```

In this case, if the value of a[i] is found to be -1, it will not be added to *total*. But, the loop will continue, so other values of a[i] might be added to *total*.

Both the *break* and *continue* statements normally work on the innermost loop. For example:

```
for (i=0; i<10; ++i) {
    for (j=0; j<10; ++j) {
        if (a[j] == -1) {
            break;
        }
        total[i] += a[j];
    }
}
```

In this case, the *break* statement will terminate the inner *for* loop, but not the outer *for* loop.

If you want to terminate both loops, you could do it by adding a label to the *break* statement, like this.

```
myLabel: for (i=0; i<10; ++i) {
    for (j=0; j<10; ++j) {
        if (a[j] == -1) {
            break myLabel;
        }
        total[i] += a[j];
    }
}
```

The name of the label (myLabel, in this example) can be any name you wish, as long as it doesn't conflict with a variable name you have used or with a Java keyword.

A label can be used on a *continue* statement in exactly the same way.

return Statements

A *return* statement serves two functions: to cause the execution of the current method to end, and to specify the value to be returned to the caller.

Here's an example of a *return* statement performing the first of those functions:

```
void print(int a,int b) {
    System.out.println("The value of a is: " + a);
    if (b == -1) {
        return;
    }
    System.out.println("The value of b is: " + b);
}
```

In this case, if *b* is -1, the method will stop executing after the first call to println, and before the second.

The second function for a *return* statement is to specify the value to be returned by a method. Here is an example of that:

```
int sum(int a,int b) {
    int c;
    c = a + b;
    if (c > 5) {
        c -= 5;
    }
    return c;
}
```

In this example, the int in the method header shows that the method should return an integer value. The *return* statement specifies what that value should be; in this case, the value is *c*. (Any expression can be used following the word *return*.)

Exception Handling Statements

If you want to execute some statements that may cause an exception (an error), you would do it as in the following example:

```
try {
    test(10);
}
catch (IllegalArgumentException e) {
    System.out.println("Illegal argument");
    return;
}
catch (IndexOutOfBoundsException e) {
    System.out.println("Index out of bounds");
    return;
}
```

77

The *try* statement identifies a block of code in which an exception may occur. Immediately following the *try* block should be one or more *catch* statements. Each *catch* statement will handle a particular kind of exception. If an exception occurs in the *try* block, and there is a *catch* block for that type of exception, the *catch* block will be executed.

An exception occurs when a *throw* statement is executed. For example, this statement would throw an IllegalArgumentException:

```
throw new IllegalArgumentException();
```

The *throw* statement must be supplied with an object which is a sub-class of Throwable. Normally, that object is generated in the *throw* statement by using the *new* operator. A number of exceptions are included in the standard Java classes, and they can be found in the Exception and RuntimeException sections in Chapter 7, "Standard Classes."

Since any sub-class of Throwable can be used in a *throw* statement, you can create your own exception classes. Normally, you would make those exceptions a sub-class of either Exception or RuntimeException (which are sub-classes of Throwable). There is an important difference between Exception and RuntimeException. If you make your exception a sub-class of RuntimeException, a method which calls your method will not be required to catch the exception. They are allowed to catch the exception, but are not required to. If they don't catch it, the standard Java exception-handling mechanism will handle it (which will cause your program to terminate with a message describing the exception). On the other hand, if you make your exception a sub-class of Exception, a method that calls your method will be required to handle it. It can handle it in one of two ways: It can include a *catch* statement for the exception, or it can list the exception in the *throws* clause of the method header. Including the exception in the *throws* clause means that your method will pass the exception back to its caller.

This example shows some methods that throw an exception:

```java
void first() {
    try {
        second();
    }
    catch (FileNotFoundException e) {
        System.out.println("Woops...");
        return;
    }
}
void second() throws FileNotFoundException {
    third();
    System.out.println("wrapping up second here...");
}
void third() throws FileNotFoundException {
    if (/* some condition */) {
        throw new FileNotFoundException();
    }
    System.out.println("wrapping up third here...");
}
```

Suppose you run this code, and the exception is thrown. Because this is not a RuntimeException, it must be handled. That means the method that throws the exception (third) is required to include the exception in the *throws* clause of the method header. When the *throw* statement executes, an immediate return from *third* takes place. (That means the System.out.println statement is never executed.) Following the return from *third,* you will be back in *second* where *third* was called. But the exception isn't handled there, either. So, another immediate return takes place. (Once again, this means the System.out.println statement will not be executed.) Now you are back in *first* where the call to *second* took place. Now the exception is finally caught, which means the code inside the *catch* statement will be executed.

If you wish, you can follow a series of *catch* statements with a *finally* statement. Here is an example:

```
try {
    second();
}
catch (FileNotFoundException e) {
    System.out.println("Woops...");
    return;
}
finally {
    file.close();
}
```

The *finally* statement includes code that is to be executed whether the *try* causes an exception or not. In many cases, such code could simply be placed after the last *catch* statement. Normally, after a *try* is executed, the code following the last catch will be executed whether the *try* was successful or not. But the above code shows one of the ways that might not happen: There is a *return* statement in the *catch* statement. That *return* would cause normal code following the last *catch* to be skipped. The *finally* statement changes that. The *finally* will be executed after the *try* and *catch* are done, even if a *return* (or another *throw*) causes a return from the method. The *finally* statement is a handy place to put clean-up code, like closing files, that you want to execute whether an exception occurs or not.

79

PART III

API Reference

CHAPTER 7

Standard Classes

This part of the book describes the standard Java™ classes, what they do, and how to use them. The classes are listed in alphabetical order, with the package name in parentheses after the class name. Preceding the class listing are Figures 7-1 through 7-5, which show the hierarchy of classes.

Table 7-1 describes these packages.

83

Table 7-1 Java packages

Package	Function
AWT	This is the largest, and most important of the standard Java packages. It includes all the classes that let you manipulate the screen, including such classes as Dialog and Graphics.
AWT.Image	This package is rather tricky, and is not of interest if all you want to do is display an image. To do that, all you need are the URL class, the *getImage* method in the Applet class, and the *drawImage* method in the Graphics class. The AWT.Image package is useful only if you want to perform manipulations of images, such as changing one color to another.
io	This package allows you to read and write files (including files accessed over the Internet).
lang	This package provides basic language features, such as a set of mathematics methods and a class to handle threads.

continued on next page

continued from previous page

Package	Function
net	This package allows you to communicate over the Internet. It contains only one class of interest to the ordinary programmer: the URL class. All the other classes are useful only if you plan to perform low-level Internet communcations.
util	This package provides various miscellaneous utility classes.

Key for Figures 7-1 through 7-5

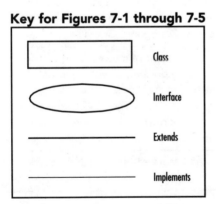

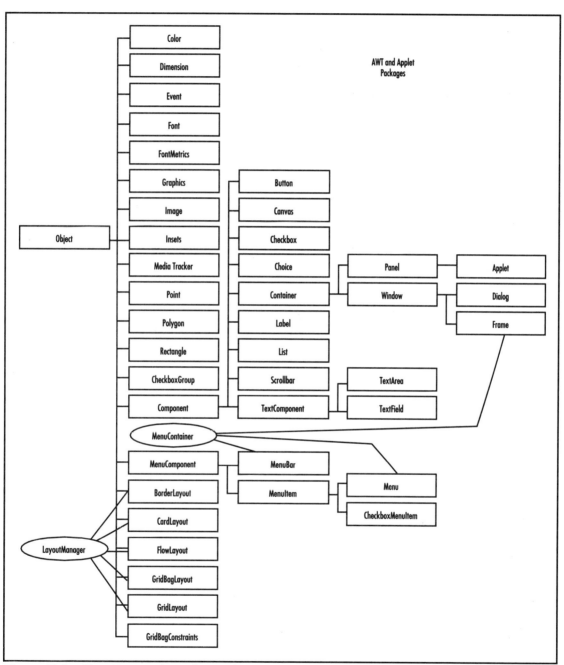

Figure 7-1 The AWT and Applet packages

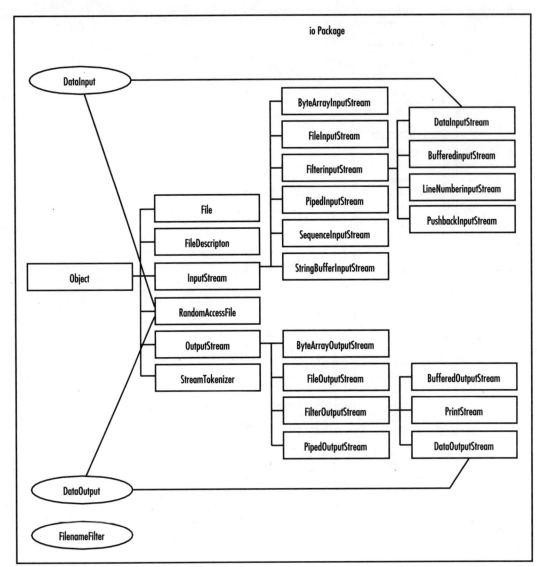

Figure 7-2 The io package

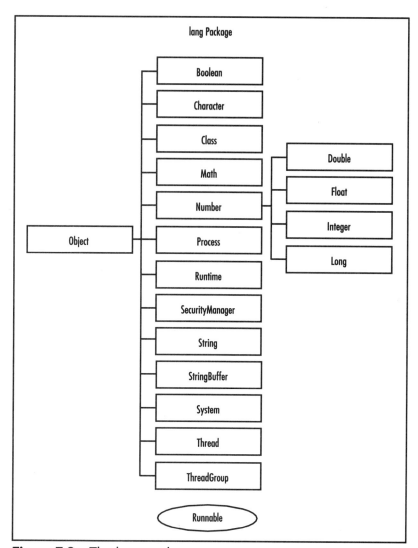

Figure 7-3 The lang package

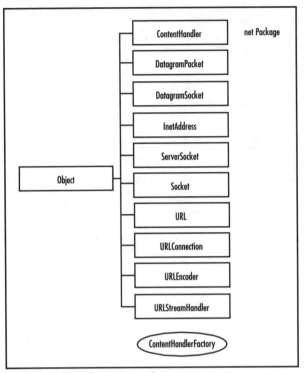

Figure 7-4   The net package

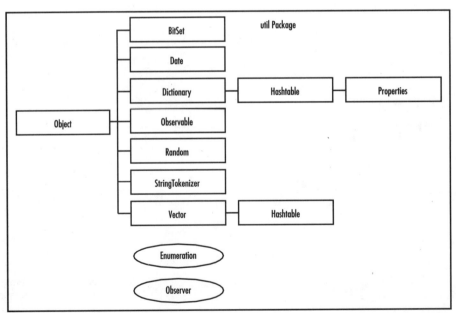

Figure 7-5   The util package

BitSet (util)

BitSet lets you create objects that represent a set of bits. You can set, clear, and test each bit individually, and you can perform logical operations on the entire set.

You can perform similar tasks with an array of boolean. The array will locate an individual element faster than a BitSet, but it will take more storage space. It also won't include the convenient methods to perform logical operations on the entire set.

```
public BitSet();
public BitSet(int nbits);
```

These constructors allow you to create BitSet objects. The first creates an object with zero bits, and the second creates one with *nbits* bits. The size of the object when you create it isn't necessarily important, since the object will grow as necessary when you use it.

```
public void set(int bit);
public void clear(int bit);
public boolean get(int bit);
```

These methods let you set (turn on), clear (turn off), and get individual bits in the set.

```
public void and(BitSet set);
public void or(BitSet set);
public void xor(BitSet set);
```

These methods let you perform logical operations on two BitSet objects. The result of the operation is placed in the object that is used to call the method.

```
public int size();
```

This method returns the number of bits currently held in the BitSet.

```
public boolean equals(Object obj);
```

This method compares two objects. To be equal, they must both be BitSet objects, and their bit values must match. If one object has more bits than the others, the extra bits must all have a value of zero for the objects to be considered equal.

```
public Object clone();
```

This method will create a copy of the BitSet object.

```
public String toString();
```

This will convert the BitSet object to a String. This can be helpful in debugging a program, especially if the String is then passed to System.out.println.

Boolean (lang)

Objects of this class are immutable. That means they are assigned a value when they are created, and that value cannot be changed later. If you want the object to have a different value, you must create a new object with that new value.

```
public static final Boolean TRUE;
public static final Boolean FALSE;
```

These are objects of the Boolean class with each of the two possible values. They can be used to compare to other objects.

```
public Boolean(boolean value);
public Boolean(String str);
```

These constructors create a new object. The parameter specifies whether the object will have a value of true or false. The *str* parameter should be true or false, and can be in either case.

```
public boolean booleanValue();
```

This returns the value of the object.

```
public static Boolean valueOf(String str);
```

This method creates a new object. The *str* parameter should be true or false, and can be in either case.

```
public String toString();
```

This converts the object to a String object which will have the value of true or false.

```
public boolean equals(Object obj);
```

This will be true if the obj is a Boolean, and if it has the same value.

```
public static boolean getBoolean(String str);
```

This is a *static* method, so it will not create a Boolean object. It will return true if the *str* is true (in upper- or lowercase).

BorderLayout (AWT)

```
public BorderLayout();
public BorderLayout(int hgap, int vgap);
```

The first constructor specifies that there should be no gap between each part of the container (such as between the South and Center parts). The second constructor allows you to specify the gap (in pixels) between each of these parts. The horizontal gap is *hgap*, and the vertical gap is *vgap*.

```
public void addLayoutComponent(String name, Component comp);
public void removeLayoutComponent(Component comp);
public void layoutContainer(Container target);
```

Although these are public methods, you shouldn't call them. Instead, you should use the *add* method of the Container class to add components to the layout.

```
public Dimension minimumLayoutSize(Container target);
public Dimension preferredLayoutSize(Container target);
```

These methods let you find out how much space the components would take if laid out in the given Container. You should call the *pack* method for the Container before calling either of these methods.

```
public String toString();
```

This will convert the BorderLayout object to a String. This can be helpful in debugging a program, especially if the *String* is then passed to System.out.println.

BufferedInputStream (io)

This class will buffer the input coming from a stream, which can greatly improve its execution speed.

One common method of using this class is by passing a new object of the FileInputStream class to the BufferedInputStream constructor. The BufferedInput-Stream object, in turn, is passed to the constructor for the DataInputStream constructor. After doing this, you would generally not use any of the methods of this class; instead, you would use the DataInputStream methods.

```
public BufferedInputStream(InputStream in);
public BufferedInputStream(InputStream in, int size);
```

These constructors allow you to create a BufferedInputStream object. The *in* is an InputStream object, often from the FileInputStream class. The *size* is the size of the buffer to be used in reading data from the stream; if you don't specify a *size*, a default value will be used.

```
public synchronized int read() throws IOException;
public synchronized int read(byte b[]) throws IOException;
public synchronized int read(byte b[], int off, int len) throws IOException;
```

These methods let you read data from the stream. The stream will read this data from its buffer, and will automatically fill the buffer as necessary to complete read requests.

The first version reads a single byte and returns it. The second version reads up to *b.length* bytes into array *b*. The third version reads up to *len* bytes into array *b* starting at index *off*. All three will return -1 if no bytes were read because the end of the stream was reached.

```
public synchronized long skip(long n) throws IOException;
```

This method skips past the next *n* characters in the stream. It returns the actual number of bytes skipped.

```
public synchronized int available() throws IOException;
```

This method returns the number of bytes which can be obtained from the stream without reading from the disk or network (this is normally the number of bytes currently in the buffer).

```
public synchronized void mark(int readlimit);
public synchronized void reset() throws IOException;
```

The *mark* method marks the current position in the stream. You can later return to that position in the stream by calling *reset*. The *readlimit* parameter specifies the maximum number of characters that can be read from the stream after the call to *mark* and before the call to *reset*. If more characters are read, the mark will be lost so a call can no longer be made to *reset*.

```
public void close() throws IOException;
```

This method closes the stream.

BufferedOutputStream (io)

This class will buffer the output going to the stream, which can greatly improve its execution speed.

One common method of using this class is that of passing a new object of the FileOutputStream class to the BufferedOutputStream constructor. The BufferedOutputStream object, in turn, is passed to the constructor for the DataOutputStream or PrintStream constructors. After doing this, you would generally not use any of the methods of this class; instead, you would use the *DataOutputStream* methods or the *PrintStream* methods.

```
public BufferedOutputStream(OutputStream out);
public BufferedOutputStream(OutputStream out, int size);
```

92

These constructors let you create a BufferedOutputStream object. The object will take data passed to it with the *write* method, and (after buffering it) send it to the out stream. If you wish, you can specify the size of the buffer to be used; if you don't, a default size will be used.

```
public synchronized void write(int b) throws IOException;
public synchronized void write(byte b[]) throws IOException;
public synchronized void write(byte b[], int off, int len) throws IOException;
```

These methods let you send data to the output stream (after residing temporarily in the buffer). The first outputs a single byte. The second outputs *b.length* bytes from array *b*. The third outputs *len* bytes from array *b* starting at index *off*.

```
public synchronized void flush() throws IOException;
```

This method writes all the data currently in the buffer to the output stream.

```
public void close() throws IOException;
```

This method closes the stream.

Button (AWT)

This class lets you create button controls. Button is a sub-class of Component, so you can use any of the *Component* methods on a Button object.

```
public Button();
public Button(String label);
```

These are the constructors. The *label* parameter is the text that appears on the button. The first constructor is of little value, since it creates a button with no text. (It would only be of value if you called setLabel at a later time to put text on the button.)

```
public String getLabel();
public void setLabel(String label);
```

These methods allow you to get and set the text that appears on the button.

ByteArrayInputStream (io)

Streams generally represent disk files, but they don't have to. They can represent any series of characters. In the ByteArrayInputStream, the stream represents a byte array.

```
public ByteArrayInputStream(byte buf[]);
public ByteArrayInputStream(byte buf[], int offset, int length);
```

These constructors let you create objects of the ByteArrayInputStream class. You must specify the array which holds the data to be used as the stream in *buf*. If you wish, you can specify a starting *offset* within that array, and the number of bytes to use in *length*.

```
public synchronized int read();
public synchronized int read(byte b[]);
public synchronized int read(byte b[], int offset, int len);
```

These methods let you read from the stream. The first method will return a single byte from the stream. The second will read up to *b.length* bytes into array *b*. The third will read up to *len* characters from the stream, and put them in array *b* starting at offset. All three methods will return -1 if no bytes were read because the end of the stream was encountered.

```
public synchronized long skip(long n);
```

This method lets you skip past *n* bytes of the stream. It returns the actual number of bytes skipped.

```
public synchronized int available();
```

This method returns the number of bytes left in the stream.

```
public synchronized void reset();
```

This method resets the processing to the beginning of the stream. (Following this, subsequent calls to read will obtain data from the beginning of the stream.)

```
public void close();
```

This method closes the stream.

ByteArrayOutputStream (io)

Streams generally represent disk files, but they don't have to. They can represent any series of characters. In the ByteArrayOutputStream, the stream represents a byte array.

```
public ByteArrayOutputStream();
public ByteArrayOutputStream(int size);
```

These constructors allow you to create an object of the ByteArrayOutputStream class. Calling these methods will create a byte array to hold the data sent to the stream. The *size* parameter specifies the initial size of the array; if you don't specify a *size,* the default will be used. It is not necessary to specify a *size* because the array will grow as necessary to hold all the data you send to it.

```
public synchronized void write(int b);
public synchronized void write(byte b[]);
public synchronized void write(byte b[], int offset, int len);
```

These methods allow you to send data to the stream. The first version sends a single byte, represented by *b*. The second sends *b.length* bytes from array *b*. The third version sends *len* bytes, which begin at index offset within array *b*.

```
public synchronized void writeTo(OutputStream out) throws IOException;
```

This method copies all the data from the stream to *out*. Note that this doesn't remove any of the data from the stream—it will still be there.

```
public synchronized void reset();
```

This method removes all the data from the stream.

```
public synchronized byte toByteArray()[];
```

This method returns a byte array that contains the data from the stream. This array is a copy of the one used to hold the stream, so you can modify it without affecting the stream.

```
public int size();
```

This method returns the number of bytes currently in the stream.

```
public String toString();
public String toString(int hibyte);
```

These methods create a String object which contains all the data from the stream. Since the data in the stream is a series of bytes, not chars, they must be converted. The first version performs this conversion by setting the high-order byte of each character to zero; the second version sets it to hibyte.

```
public void close() throws IOException;
public void flush() throws IOException;
```

These methods are provided because they are standard *OutputStream* methods, but they perform no processing.

Canvas (AWT)

Canvas is a sub-class of Component, so you can use any of the *Component* methods on a Canvas object.

A Canvas object isn't very useful by itself, but it can be sub-classed to create a customized control or a special portion of a frame. The Canvas sub-class can have its own *paint* method to draw itself, and can handle any events sent to it. It has no special methods of its own.

CardLayout (AWT)

This class lets you create objects that perform card layout. That means they display only one of the components in the container at a time, letting you switch between them like cards.

```
public CardLayout();
public CardLayout(int hgap, int vgap);
```

The first constructor specifies that there should be no gap around the outside edge of the container. The second constructor allows you to specify the gap (in pixels). *hgap* is the horizontal gap (the gap on the top and bottom edges), and *vgap* is the vertical gap (the gap on the left and right edges).

```
public void addLayoutComponent(String name, Component comp);
public void removeLayoutComponent(Component comp);
public void layoutContainer(Container target);
```

Although these are public methods, you shouldn't call them. Instead, you should use the *add* method of the Container class to add components to the layout.

```
public Dimension minimumLayoutSize(Container target);
public Dimension preferredLayoutSize(Container target);
```

These methods let you find out how much space the components would take if laid out in the given Container. You should call the *pack* method for the Container before calling either of these methods.

```
public void first(Container parent);
public void next(Container parent);
public void previous(Container parent);
public void last(Container parent);
public void show(Container parent, String name);
```

These methods allow you to select which of the Components is displayed. (Only one is displayed at a time.) The parent is the Container being laid out (usually a Dialog or Panel). The name would be the name given to the Component when it was added to the layout by calling the *add* method.

```
public String toString();
```

This will convert the CardLayout object to a String. This can be helpful in debugging a program, especially if the String is then passed to System.out.println.

Character (lang)

Objects of this class are immutable. That means they are assigned a value when they are created, and that value cannot be changed later. If you want the object to have a different value, you must create a new object with that new value.

Notice that the class is spelled Character, not Char. Also notice that many of the methods in this class are *static*, and thus don't involve creating a Character object.

```
public static final int MIN_RADIX;
public static final int MAX_RADIX;
```

These are the minimum and maximum values that can be used for the *radix* parameter in the *digit* and *forDigit* methods.

```
public static boolean isLowerCase(char ch);
public static boolean isUpperCase(char ch);
public static boolean isDigit(char ch);
public static boolean isSpace(char ch);
```

The methods return true if the character is of the given type. Note that *isSpace* will be true for any whitespace character, including space, tab, return, new line, or form feed.

```
public static char toLowerCase(char ch);
public static char toUpperCase(char ch);
```

These methods convert the character to the specified case.

```
public static int digit(char ch, int radix);
public static char forDigit(int digit, int radix);
```

These methods let you convert between characters which hold a digit, and integers. (If the digit passed to *forDigit* is too large to be a single digit, zero is returned.)

```
public Character(char value);
```

This method is the constructor.

```
public boolean equals(Object obj);
```

This method returns true if obj is a Character and if it has the same value.

```
public String toString();
```

This converts the Character to a String.

Checkbox (AWT)

This class lets you create checkboxes and radio buttons.

Checkbox is a sub-class of Component, so you can use any of the *Component* methods on a Checkbox object.

```
public Checkbox();
public Checkbox(String label);
public Checkbox(String label, CheckboxGroup group, boolean state);
```

The first two constructors create a regular checkbox. The third creates a grouped checkbox—what Windows calls a radio button.

Before creating a grouped checkbox, you need to create a CheckboxGroup object, and pass that object to the constructor. Normally, several such checkboxes will share the same CheckboxGroup object. One of those checkboxes will be selected—it should have true for its *state* parameter. The other checkboxes should have false for that parameter.

The label is the text which appears next to the checkbox.

```
public String getLabel();
public void setLabel(String label);
```

These methods let you get and set the text which appears next to the checkbox.

```
public boolean getState();
```

This method returns true if the checkbox is currently checked, or false if not. It can be used with both "regular" and "grouped" checkboxes.

```
public void setState(boolean state);
```

This method lets you change the state of the checkbox. With regular checkboxes, you can pass either true or false for the state, and this will turn the checkbox on or off. With grouped checkboxes, you can only pass true, which will select this checkbox (and de-select the other checkboxes in the same group).

```
public CheckboxGroup getCheckboxGroup();
public void setCheckboxGroup(CheckboxGroup g);
```

These methods allow you to set and get the CheckboxGroup object associated with the checkbox. (Setting the CheckboxGroup object is normally done in the constructor, but can also be done with *set*CheckboxGroup.)

CheckboxGroup (AWT)

This class lets you create an object which groups together a series of Checkbox objects. Doing this insures that only one of the Checkbox objects is selected at once, and causes the objects to be displayed as radio buttons rather than ordinary checkboxes.

```
public CheckboxGroup();
```

This constructor lets you create CheckboxGroup objects.

```
public Checkbox getCurrent();
public synchronized void setCurrent(Checkbox box);
```

These methods allow you to set and get which checkbox is currently selected.

```
public String toString();
```

This will convert the CheckboxGroup object to a String. This can be helpful in debugging a program, especially if the String is then passed to System.out.println.

CheckboxMenuItem (AWT)

This class is a sub-class of MenuComponent, so you can use the methods from that class as well as those listed below when operating on a CheckboxMenuItem object.

Remember the hierarchy for menu classes: The highest level is a MenuBar. There will be just one of those objects in a frame at a time. That object references a series of Menu objects (e.g., a Menu object for the File menu, one for the Edit menu, etc.). Each Menu object references a series of MenuItem objects (e.g., a MenuItem object for Open, one for New, one for Save, etc.).

Items of the CheckboxMenuItem class can be used in place of MenuItem objects if the item is to be checkable.

```
public CheckboxMenuItem(String label);
```

This constructor will create a CheckboxMenuItem with the given label displayed on the menu.

```
public boolean getState();
public void setState(boolean t);
```

These methods allow you to get and set the state (i.e., whether or not a checkmark appears next to the menu item). A CheckboxMenuItem is automatically unchecked when it is first created.

Choice (AWT)

98

This class lets you create Choice controls. They are the kind of control called a drop-down combo box by Windows.

Choice is a sub-class of Component, so you can use any of the *Component* methods on a Choice object.

```
public Choice();
```

The constructor

```
public int countItems();
```

returns the number of items in the choice control.

```
public String getItem(int index);
```

This returns the text for the given item in the control. Use an index of zero for the first item, one for the second, and so forth.

```
public synchronized void addItem(String item);
```

This method adds an item to the end of the list in the control. (Because you can only add to the end of the list, you must call addItem in the order you want the items to appear in the control.)

```
public String getSelectedItem();
public int getSelectedIndex();
```

These methods allow you to determine which of the items in the control is current-ly selected. The first method returns the text for the item, and the second returns the index. (The index will be zero for the first item, one for the second, and so forth.)

```
public synchronized void select(int pos);
public void select(String str);
```

These methods allow you to choose which item in the control is currently selected. The first method uses an index, which would be zero to select the first item, one to select the second, and so on. The second method selects the item with the given text. (It will have no effect if none of the items have that text.)

Class (lang)

Yes, there really is a class named Class. At runtime, one object of this class will be cre-ated for each class the program uses. While this is useful to the Java runtime software, it has little value to you as a programmer.

```
public static native Class forName(String className) throws ClassNotFoundException;
public native Object newInstance()  throws InstantiationException, IllegalAccessException;
public native String getName();
public native Class getSuperclass();
public native Class getInterfaces()[];
public native ClassLoader getClassLoader();
public native boolean isInterface();
public String toString();
```

99

Color (AWT)

This class can be used to create Color objects which are used as parameters to various other Java methods (such as the *setColor* method in the Graphics class).

```
public final static Color white;
public final static Color lightGray;
public final static Color gray;
public final static Color darkGray;
public final static Color black;
public final static Color red;
public final static Color pink;
public final static Color orange;
public final static Color yellow;
public final static Color green;
public final static Color magenta;
public final static Color cyan;
public final static Color blue;
```

These static Color objects are very handy for use in passing as parameters to meth-ods (such as the *setColor* method in the Graphics class).

```
public Color(int r, int g, int b);
public Color(int rgb);
public Color(float r, float g, float b);
```

These constructors let you create a new Color object.

The first version lets you specify the red, green, and blue components of the new color as three integers. Each should be in the 0 to 255 range.

The second version lets you specify the red, green, and blue components combined into a single integer. The high-order 8 bits of the integer are ignored. The next 8 bits should be the red value. The next 8 bits should be the green value. And the last 8 bits should be the blue value. Each value can range from 0 to 255.

The third version lets you specify the red, green, and blue components as three floating-point values in the range 0 to 1.

```
public int getRed();
public int getGreen();
public int getBlue();
public int getRGB();
```

These methods let you get information about the color. The first three return one component of the color, which will be in the range 0 to 255.

The last method returns the color combined into a single integer. The high-order 8 bits will be 0xff. The next 8 bits will be the red value. The next 8 bits will be the green value. The last 8 bits will be the blue value. Each of the three values will be in the range from 0 to 255.

```
public Color brighter();
public Color darker();
```

These methods will make the color slightly brighter or darker.

```
public static int HSBtoRGB(float hue, float saturation, float brightness);
```

This method allows you to create an integer containing a color, and lets you specify the color using the hue/saturation/brightness system. Each of the three components should be in the range 0 to 1. The resulting integer will have the combined color, just as it would be passed to the second constructor (listed above).

```
public static float[] RGBtoHSB(int r, int g, int b, float[] hsbvals);
```

This method will convert a color specified by its red/green/blue components into a color specified using hue/saturation/brightness. The resulting array will have three elements ranging from 0 to 1, which provide the hue, saturation, and brightness values.

```
public static Color getHSBColor(float h, float s, float b);
```

This method will create a new Color object based on the supplied hue, saturation, and brightness values. Each value should be in the 0 to 1 range.

ColorModel (AWT.Image)

This method is the super-class to the DirectColorModel and IndexColorModel classes. Although it provides a couple of methods of its own, its main function is to group together those other two classes.

```
public ColorModel(int bits);
public int getPixelSize();
public int getRGB(int pixel)
```

Component (AWT)

This is probably the most important class in the AWT package. All of the controls (checkboxes, scrollbars, etc.) are sub-classes of Component, as are Dialog, Frame, and Panel. That means that the methods in this class can be used on a variety of AWT objects.

Although Component is an important class, you never create objects of this class. Instead, you create objects of one of its sub-classes.

```
public Container getParent();
```

This method tells you where the Component is located. This is usually a Frame, Dialog, or Panel object.

```
public boolean isVisible();
public synchronized void show();
public void show(boolean cond);
public synchronized void hide();
```

A component can be either visible or invisible. You can use these methods to control and test the visiblity of a component..Controls are visible by default. Dialogs and Frames are invisible by default.

```
public boolean isShowing();
```

This tells you if the component is in a container that is currently active. For example, if you create a control and put it in a dialog, the *isShowing* value will become true as soon as you show the dialog. If you later dispose the dialog, the *isShowing* value will become false.

```
public boolean isEnabled();
public synchronized void enable();
public void enable(boolean cond);
public synchronized void disable();
```

A component can be either enabled or disabled. If it is disabled, it will be visible on the screen, but cannot be operated by the user. (This is normally used for controls, not for dialogs or frames.) These methods let you control and test whether a control is enabled.

```
public Point location();
public Dimension size();
public Rectangle bounds();
```

These methods let you determine the location and size of the component. The coordinates are always relative to the component's parent. (For example, if you use location on a control that is in a dialog, you'll get its location relative to the upper left-hand corner of the dialog.)

```
public Color getForeground();
public synchronized void setForeground(Color c);
public Color getBackground();
public synchronized void setBackground(Color c);
```

Each component has two colors: a foreground color and a background color. The foreground color is used to draw text, and the background color is used to fill the space behind the text. (Other colors may also be used, depending upon the component.)

```
public Font getFont();
public synchronized void setFont(Font f);
```

These methods let you set and get the font that is used for the component. This is useful mainly for frames, since controls look best with the default font.

```
public void move(int x, int y);
public void resize(int width, int height);
public void resize(Dimension d);
public synchronized void reshape(int x, int y, int width, int height);
```

These methods allow you to move the component to a different location. The coordinates are always relative to the component's parent. For example, if you are working with a control that is in a dialog, the coordinates you would use are relative to the upper left-hand corner of the dialog.

```
public Dimension preferredSize();
public Dimension minimumSize();
```

These methods return the preferred and minimum size for the component. (Remember that a component's size may change, and will often be controlled by a layout manager. The layout manager uses these methods to determine how large a component must be, and to try to find room for its preferred size.)

```
public Graphics getGraphics();
```

This obtains a Graphics object for the component. This object can be used to draw to the component. (You wouldn't normally do that. You would draw only in a *paint* or *update* method, and use the Graphics object that is passed to the method as a parameter.)

```
public FontMetrics getFontMetrics(Font font);
```

This method obtains a FontMetrics object for the specified font. (That object allows you to determine things like the height of the font.)

```
public void paint(Graphics g);
public void update(Graphics g);
```

The *paint* and *update* methods are called whenever the component needs to be drawn on the screen.

If the component is a frame, you would commonly create a Frame sub-class and override the *paint* method in the sub-class. That allows you to draw to the frame.

You might also override *update*, although that is less common. *update* is responsible for erasing the background and then calling *paint*. Since the version of *update* in the Component class does that, you don't normally need to override it. (The most common reason to override it is if you are using double-buffering to perform some animation.)

```
public void repaint();
public void repaint(long tm);
public void repaint(int x, int y, int width, int height);
public void repaint(long tm, int x, int y, int width, int height);
```

These methods cause a call to *update* (which then calls *paint*) to be made. The call to *update* may not happen right away. Instead, Java queues the request for the call to *update*, and will handle it.

If you supply the *tm* parameter, the call to *update* should happen within that number of milliseconds. This is just a request to the system, and cannot be guaranteed.

If you supply *x, y, width,* and *height*, only the part of the component that you specify by those parameters will actually be redrawn—the rest of the component will remain as it is. If you don't supply those parameters, the entire component will be redrawn.

```
public boolean imageUpdate(Image img, int flags, int x, int y, int w, int h);
public Image createImage(ImageProducer producer)
public Image createImage(int width, int height);
public boolean prepareImage(Image image, ImageObserver observer);
public boolean prepareImage(Image image, int width, int height, ImageObserver observer);
public int checkImage(Image image, ImageObserver observer);
public int checkImage(Image image, int width, int height, ImageObserver observer);
```

If you read an image from the Internet, the image generally takes some time to download. During that time, your applet continues to run, but leaves an empty space where the image will be displayed. Then, as the image arrives, it will be drawn in the appropriate location. These methods let Java provide that functionality. Although you can use them directly to create software that generates images, they are generally useful only to the standard Java methods.

103

```
public synchronized boolean inside(int x, int y);
```

This method tells you if the specified coordinates are within the component. The coordinates are relative to the component's parent. For example, if you were testing to see if a point was inside a button on a dialog, you would use coordinates relative to the upper left-hand corner of the dialog.

```
public void deliverEvent(Event e);
public boolean postEvent(Event e);
```

These methods both do the same thing—they cause the specified event to be handled by the component. They do this by calling the *handleEvent* method for the component. (You would not normally call these methods yourself. Since events are generated and passed to *handleEvent* by Java. But, if you wanted to pass an event you had received to another component, or if you wanted to synthetically create an event, you could use these methods to cause the event to be handled.)

```
public boolean handleEvent(Event evt);
public boolean mouseDown(Event evt, int x, int y);
public boolean mouseDrag(Event evt, int x, int y);
public boolean mouseUp(Event evt, int x, int y);
```

continued on next page

continued from previous page

```
public boolean mouseMove(Event evt, int x, int y);
public boolean mouseEnter(Event evt, int x, int y);
public boolean mouseExit(Event evt, int x, int y);
public boolean keyDown(Event evt, int key);
public boolean keyUp(Event evt, int key);
public boolean action(Event evt, Object what);
public boolean gotFocus(Event evt, Object what);
public boolean lostFocus(Event evt, Object what);
```

When an event occurs, it is passed to *handleEvent*. It will, in turn, pass most events to one of the other event methods listed here. If you create a frame or dialog, you will normally sub-class the Frame or Dialog class. Within that sub-class, you can override one or more of these methods, which allows you to handle these events.

If you override *handleEvent* it is important that you call the super-class version with super.handleEvent(evt) to insure that events are routed properly. (This is not necessary for any of the other event methods.)

```
public void requestFocus();
public void nextFocus();
```

These events allow you to request that a certain component be given the focus, or that the focus be passed to the next logical component. The component with the focus is the one the user is currently operating. Because of this, it will be the one to receive most keyboard events.

This method can be used on controls, dialogs, and frames. When used on a dialog or frame, it will generally make it the topmost window (although there are certain restrictions, e.g., modal dialogs will always remain on top).

```
public String toString();
```

This will convert the Component object to a String. This can be helpful in debugging a program, especially if the String is then passed to System.out.println.

104

Container (AWT)

You can't create objects of this class, but you can create objects of several of its sub-classes: Panel, Dialog, Frame, and Applet. Those sub-classes all contain various components (e.g., a Dialog object might contain a number of controls, such as Button and Choice objects). This class provides those sub-classes with the ability to group together a series of Component objects.

Most of the methods for this class are used internally by Java and are of little value when writing applications or applets. The two very notable exceptions are *add*, which you use to add components to the container, and *setLayout*, which you can use to select the layout manager.

```
public int countComponents();
```

Returns the number of components in the container.

```
public synchronized Component getComponent(int n);
public synchronized Component[] getComponents();
```

These methods let you obtain a single component from the container, or all the components.

```
public Insets insets();
```

This method obtains the Insets object for the container. It indicates how much empty space is to be left surrounding the container. (This leaves room for things like the title bar on a dialog box.)

```
public Component add(Component comp);
public synchronized Component add(String name, Component comp);
public synchronized Component add(Component comp, int pos);
public synchronized void remove(Component comp);
public synchronized void removeAll();
```

These methods let you add and remove components from the container. For most layout managers, you can use the first and third methods to add a component. For the BorderLayout manager, you should use the second method, since it provides the name that indicates the border for the component. You can also use the second method with the CardLayout manager if you plan to reference the cards by name.

```
public LayoutManager getLayout();
public void setLayout(LayoutManager mgr);
```

These methods let you get and set the layout manager. It will determine where the components are placed in the container, and how large each should be.

By default, the layout manager for Dialog and Frame objects is BorderLayout, and the default for Panel objects is FlowLayout.

```
public synchronized Dimension preferredSize();
public synchronized Dimension minimumSize();
```

These methods return the preferred and minimum size for the container. Those sizes are used by the layout manager if the container is within another container.

```
public Component locate(int x, int y);
```

This method lets you find the Component object located at the given coordinates.

ContentHandler (net)

This class reads a stream of data (such as a .gif file) and creates an object from it (such as an Image object). This happens behind the scenes, and you would never need to use this class directly.

ContentHandlerFactory (net)

This class creates ContentHandler objects. This happens behind the scenes, and you would never need to use this class directly.

CropImageFilter (AWT.Image)

This is one of two standard Java classes which can filter an image (i.e., which are sub-classes of ImageFilter). This filter crops the image (i.e., removes all but a rectangular area within the image). This class would not be used directly in a program which is simply displaying an image; like most of the classes in AWT.Image, it is used only for the unusual case in which image manipulation is to be done.

```
public CropImageFilter(int x, int y, int w, int h);
public void setProperties(Hashtable props);
public void setDimensions(int w, int h);
public void setPixels(int x, int y, int w, int h, ColorModel model, byte pixels[], ⇐
int off, int scansize);
public void setPixels(int x, int y, int w, int h, ColorModel model, int pixels[], ⇐
int off, int scansize);
```

DatagramPacket (net)

This class defines the packets used by the DatagramSocket class. This is a low-level function that you would not normally use directly.

```
public DatagramPacket(byte ibuf[], int ilength);
public DatagramPacket(byte ibuf[], int ilength, InetAddress iaddr, int iport);
public InetAddress getAddress();
public int getPort();
public byte[] getData();
public int getLength();
```

DatagramSocket (net)

This class allows you to send and receive datagrams over the Internet. This is a low-level function that you would not normally use directly.

```
public DatagramSocket() throws SocketException;
public DatagramSocket(int port) throws SocketException;
public void send(DatagramPacket p) throws IOException;
public synchronized void receive(DatagramPacket p) throws IOException;
public int getLocalPort();
public synchronized void close();
```

DataInputStream (io)

The DataInputStream class acts much like other InputStream objects: It lets you read a series of characters in order. The difference is that this class lets you treat that series of characters as a series of data items. Those data items might be ints, Strings, or any of several other data types.

You create an object of this class by passing the constructor another InputStream object—most commonly, either a FileInputStream or a BufferedInputStream (and the BufferedInputStream is, in turn, based on a FileInputStream object).

```
public DataInputStream(InputStream in);
```

This constructor lets you create a DataInputStream object. It can take any InputStream object as a parameter, but most commonly it uses either a FileInputStream or BufferedInputStream object.

```
public final int read(byte b[]) throws IOException;
public final int read(byte b[], int off, int len) throws IOException;
public final void readFully(byte b[]) throws IOException;
public final void readFully(byte b[], int off, int len) throws IOException;
public final boolean readBoolean() throws IOException;
public final byte readByte() throws IOException;
public final int readUnsignedByte() throws IOException;
public final short readShort() throws IOException;
public final int readUnsignedShort() throws IOException;
public final char readChar() throws IOException;
public final int readInt() throws IOException;
public final long readLong() throws IOException;
public final float readFloat() throws IOException;
public final double readDouble() throws IOException;
public final String readLine() throws IOException;
public final static String readUTF(DataInput in) throws IOException;
```

These methods let you read data from the stream. To insure that the data is in the proper form, it is best to read it using the method that corresponds to the one the data was written with. For example, if a certain part of the stream was written with the *writeLong* method in the DataOutputStream class, then you would read it with *readLong*. (Other methods might work, but are not guaranteed.)

107

The first two methods will not necessarily read either all the bytes in the stream, or the number of bytes you have asked for. They may, in fact, just read the number of bytes that happen to be on hand. The actual number of bytes read will be returned by the method. If you want to be sure of reading either the number of bytes you have asked for, or all the bytes in the stream, you should use the *readFully* methods.

The *readUTF* method reads character data which has been written in the special UTF format. This format places data in a form in which Latin characters take just one byte, rather than the two that a Unicode character takes. The tradeoff for this savings is that non-Latin characters (such as Chinese characters) may take more than the two bytes a Unicode character normally takes. There is a *writeUTF* method in the DataOutputStream class which will create data in this format.

The first two methods will return -1 if the end of the stream is reached without locating any data. The remaining methods will throw an EOFException if the end of the stream is reached before the amount of data needed to fulfill the request is read.

```
public final int skipBytes(int n) throws IOException;
```

This method will cause the next *n* bytes in the stream to be skipped. It returns the actual number of bytes skipped.

```
public int available() throws IOException;
```

This method returns the number of bytes which can be obtained from the stream without having to perform a disk or network read operation.

```
public void close() throws IOException;
```

This method closes the stream.

DataOutputStream (io)

The DataOutputStream class acts much like other OutputStream objects: It lets you write a series of bytes in order. The difference is that this class lets you treat that series of bytes as a series of data items. Those data items might be ints, doubles, or any of several other data types.

You create an object of this class by passing the constructor another OutputStream object—most commonly either a FileOutputStream or a BufferedOutputStream (and the BufferedOutputStream is, in turn, based on a FileOutputStream object.)

```
public DataOutputStream(OutputStream out);
```

This constructor lets you create a DataOutputStream object. It can take any Output-Stream object as a parameter, but most commonly it uses either FileOutputStream or BufferedOutputStream objects.

108

```
public final void write(int i) throws IOException;
public final void write(byte b[]) throws IOException;
public final void write(byte b[], int off, int len) throws IOException;
public final void writeBoolean(boolean v) throws IOException;
public final void writeByte(int v) throws IOException;
public final void writeShort(int v) throws IOException;
public final void writeChar(int v) throws IOException;
public final void writeInt(int v) throws IOException;
public final void writeLong(long v) throws IOException;
public final void writeFloat(float v) throws IOException;
public final void writeDouble(double v) throws IOException;
public final void writeBytes(String s) throws IOException;
public final void writeChars(String s) throws IOException;
public final void writeUTF(String str) throws IOException;
```

These methods let you write data to the stream. You can later read the data by using the corresponding method in the DataInputStream class. For example, if a certain part of the stream was written with the *writeLong* method in the DataOutputStream class, then you would read it with *readLong*. (Other methods might work, but are not guaranteed.)

The first method writes a single byte to the stream. The second writes *b.length* bytes from array *b*. The third writes *len* bytes from array *b* starting at index *off*.

The *writeUTF* method writes character data in the special UTF format. This format places data in a form in which Latin characters take just one byte, rather than the two that a Unicode character takes. The tradeoff for this savings is that non-Latin characters (such as Chinese characters) may take more than the two bytes that a Unicode character normally takes. There is a *readUTF* method in the DataInputStream class which will read data in this format.

```
public void flush() throws IOException;
```

This method "flushes" the buffer by writing all the accumulated data from the buffer to the data file.

```
public final int size();
```

This method returns the total number of bytes written to the stream so far.

```
public void close() throws IOException;
```

This method closes the stream.

Date (util)

The Date class lets you create objects that represent a particular time on a particular date.

```
public Date();
public Date(long date);
public Date(String s);
public Date(int year, int month, int date);
public Date(int year, int month, int date, int hrs, int min);
public Date(int year, int month, int date, int hrs, int min, int sec);
```

These constructors let you create a Date object.

The first version creates an object that represents the current date and time.

The second version creates an object that represents the time date milliseconds since midnight on January 1, 1970.

The third version creates an object that represents the date in the *str*. Different string formats are valid, including ones like "12 Aug 1995 13:30:00".

The remaining versions create an object with the specified date and time. The year should be passed as the number of years since 1900 (e.g., use 110, not 2010). The month should be in the range 0 to 11. The day should be in the range 1 to 31. The hour should be in the range 0 to 23. The minute should be in the range 0 to 59. The second should be in the range 0 to 59. Some variations on those ranges are allowed. For example, if you specify a day of 32 for a month of 0, it will be translated to February 1 (not January 32).

```
public static long UTC(int year, int month, int date, int hrs, int min, int sec);
```

This returns the date in the Universal Coordinated Time format. In this format, the four low-order decimal digits represent the number of seconds since midnight, and the remaining digits represent the number of days since January 1, 1970.

```
public static long parse(String s);
```

This will convert a string containing a time into the number of milliseconds since January 1, 1970. Different string formats are valid, including ones like "12 Aug 1995 13:30:00".

```
public int getYear();
public void setYear(int year);
public int getMonth();
public void setMonth(int month);
public int getDate();
public void setDate(int date);
public int getHours();
public void setHours(int hours);
public int getMinutes();
public void setMinutes(int minutes);
public int getSeconds();
public void setSeconds(int seconds);
```

These methods let you get and set the different parts of the date and time. Remember that the year is expressed in years since 1900 (so 2010 is 110), and the month is expressed in the range 0 to 11, not 1 to 12.

```
public int getDay();
```

This returns the day of the week, with zero meaning Sunday, 1 meaning Monday, and so on.

110

```
public long getTime();
public void setTime(long time);
```

This lets you get and set the time in terms of milliseconds since January 1, 1970.

```
public boolean before(Date when);
public boolean after(Date when);
public boolean equals(Object when);
```

These methods will compare two Date objects. The first will be true if the object calling the method is earlier than *when*. The second will be true if the object is later than *when*. The third will be true if the object is for the same time as *when*.

```
public native String toString();
public native String toGMTString();
public native String toLocaleString();
```

These methods convert the date to various String formats. The first will be like "Sat Jan 15 17:05:32 1996". The second will be like "15 Jan 1996 23:05:32 GMT". The format of the third will vary from platform to platform, and depending upon how the parameters on your system are set. An example from a Windows system is "01/15/96 17:05:32".

Notice that the second method shows the time in the GMT time zone, but the other two show it in your local time zone.

```
public int getTimezoneOffset();
```

This method returns the number of minutes difference between your time zone and Greenwich Mean Time.

Dialog (AWT)

Dialog is a sub-class of Container, Window, and Component, so you can use methods from any of those classes, as well as those listed below, to control a Dialog object.

```
public Dialog(Frame parent, boolean modal);
public Dialog(Frame parent, String title, boolean modal);
```

These constructors let you create a Dialog object.

The *parent* parameter indicates the frame the dialog belongs to. Although *parent* can be *null*, this causes the dialog to be created as an independent task, which is not normally what you want.

The *modal* parameter specifies whether the dialog is to be modal. (A modal dialog is one which the user must terminate before continuing to perform other processing in the other windows of the program.)

The *title* parameter specifies the title displayed in the dialog box. If you don't specify a title, the dialog will be untitled (which usually means untitled will appear at the top of the dialog box).

```
public boolean isModal()
```

This method tells you whether or not the dialog is modal.

```
public String getTitle();
public void setTitle(String title);
```

These methods let you get and set the title displayed at the top of the dialog box.

```
public boolean isResizable();
public void setResizable(boolean resizable);
```

These methods let you set and get the option that controls resizing of the dialog box. By default, dialog boxes can be resized, but you can turn this ability off with setResizable.

Dimension (AWT)

These objects are returned by various Java class methods, and can be passed as parameters to a few of them. They simply specify the height and width of something. (What that something is depends upon the context in which the object is being used.)

```
public int width;
public int height;
```

These are the two field variables within the object.

```
public Dimension();
public Dimension(Dimension d);
public Dimension(int width, int height);
```

These constructors allow you to create a Dimension object. The first version sets the height and width to zero. The others set the height and width to the values passed as parameters.

```
public String toString();
```

This will convert the Dimension object to a String. This can be helpful in debugging a program, especially if the String is then passed to System.out.println.

DirectColorModel (AWT.Image)

This class describes a method of storing color in pixels in which each pixel contains the red, green, and blue components of its color. This class would not be used directly in a program which is simply displaying an image; like most of the classes in AWT.Image, it is used only for the unusual case in which image manipulation is to be done.

```
public DirectColorModel(int bits, int rmask, int gmask, int bmask);
public DirectColorModel(int bits, int rmask, int gmask, int bmask, int amask);
final public int getRedMask();
final public int getGreenMask();
final public int getBlueMask();
final public int getAlphaMask();
final public int getRed(int pixel);
final public int getGreen(int pixel);
final public int getBlue(int pixel);
final public int getAlpha(int pixel);
final public int getRGB(int pixel);
```

112

Double (lang)

Objects of this class are immutable. That means they are assigned a value when they are created, and that value cannot be changed later. If you want the object to have a different value, you must create a new object with that new value.

```
public static final double POSITIVE_INFINITY;
public static final double NEGATIVE_INFINITY;
public static final double NaN;
public static final double MAX_VALUE;
public static final double MIN_VALUE;
```

IEEE specs allow a floating point number to have a few special values. Those values are listed here, and can be used to compare against *double* variables.

```
public Double(double value);
public Double(String s) throws NumberFormatException;
```

These constructors allow you to create a *Double*.

```
public static native String toString(double d);
```

This converts a *double* to a String.

```
public static native Double valueOf(String s) throws NumberFormatException;
```

This converts a String to a *Double*.

```
static public boolean isNaN(double v);
static public boolean isInfinite(double v);
```

These methods return true if the value is not a number or is infinite.

```
public boolean isNaN();
public boolean isInfinite();
```

These methods return true if the object is not a number or is infinite.

```
public String toString();
public int intValue();
public long longValue();
public float floatValue();
public double doubleValue();
```

This converts the *Double* to other types.

```
public boolean equals(Object obj);
```

This returns true if the obj is a *Double*, and if it has the same numeric value.

```
public static native long doubleToLongBits(double value);
public static native double longBitsToDouble(long bits);
```

These allow you to copy a sequence of bits that are stored in a *long* to a location that is treated as a *double*, and vice versa. No conversion is performed here. The bits are simply copied from one location to another and assumed to be in the proper format.

113

Enumeration (util)

This interface specifies the methods a class must provide to allow you to list all the items in a set. For example, if you had a collection of objects of a certain type, and you wanted to be able to perform some processing on each of them, you might create a class which implements Enumeration. That class would allow you to retrieve each of the objects, one at a time, so you could process them.

```
boolean hasMoreElements();
```

This method returns true if there are more objects to be processed, or false if not. If it returns true, that means you can call nextElement at least one more time.

```
Object nextElement();
```

You call this method over and over, retrieving the next object in the list each time. You should call hasMoreElements before each time you call nextElement to insure that there are more elements in the list.

Event (AWT)

Objects of this class are created by Java, and passed to various event-handling methods (primarily in the *Component* class).

```
public static final int SHIFT_MASK;
public static final int CTRL_MASK;
public static final int META_MASK;
public static final int ALT_MASK;
```

These values can be used to determine if the specified key was held down during the event. For example, if you have an Event object named *e*, the expression *e*.modifiers & *Event.SHIFT_MASK* tells you if the <SHIFT> key was held down. For <SHIFT> and <CTRL>, it is generally easier to use the *shiftDown* and *controlDown* methods.

The META_MASK refers to a key not found on PC keyboards, but found on other keyboards (such as those for a Macintosh).

These masks are also used for mouse events. The META_MASK means the right mouse button was pressed, and the ALT_MASK means the center button was pressed.

```
public static final int HOME;
public static final int END;
public static final int PGUP;
public static final int PGDN;
public static final int UP;
public static final int DOWN;
public static final int LEFT;
public static final int RIGHT;
public static final int F1;
public static final int F2;
public static final int F3;
public static final int F4;
public static final int F5;
public static final int F6;
public static final int F7;
public static final int F8;
public static final int F9;
public static final int F10;
public static final int F11;
public static final int F12;
```

114

These values are placed in the *key* field variable when the user presses a special key. In that case, the *id* field will be either Event.KEY_ACTION or Event.KEY_ACTION_RELEASE, rather than Event.KEY_PRESS or Event.KEY_RELEASE.

```
public static final int WINDOW_DESTROY;
public static final int WINDOW_EXPOSE;
public static final int WINDOW_ICONIFY;
public static final int WINDOW_DEICONIFY;
public static final int WINDOW_MOVED;
public static final int KEY_PRESS;
public static final int KEY_RELEASE;
public static final int KEY_ACTION;
```

```
public static final int KEY_ACTION_RELEASE;
public static final int MOUSE_DOWN;
public static final int MOUSE_UP;
public static final int MOUSE_MOVE;
public static final int MOUSE_ENTER;
public static final int MOUSE_EXIT;
public static final int MOUSE_DRAG;
public static final int SCROLL_LINE_UP;
public static final int SCROLL_LINE_DOWN;
public static final int SCROLL_PAGE_UP;
public static final int SCROLL_PAGE_DOWN;
public static final int SCROLL_ABSOLUTE;
public static final int LIST_SELECT;
public static final int LIST_DESELECT;
public static final int ACTION_EVENT;
public static final int LOAD_FILE;
public static final int SAVE_FILE;
public static final int GOT_FOCUS;
public static final int LOST_FOCUS;
```

These are the values which can be found in the *id* field variable.

```
public Object target;
```

This is the object which was involved in the event. For example, if the mouse was pressed down in a control, this would be the control.

```
public long when;
```

This is the time at which the event occurred, measured as the number of milliseconds since January 1, 1970. (This is a convenient way to store the time because it can be used to create an object of the *Date* class.)

```
public int id;
```

This identifies the type of event that occurred. It is one of the static variables listed above.

```
public int x;
public int y;
```

These fields identify the point at which the event took place. For some events, such as Event.GOT_FOCUS, this isn't meaningful. It is useful mainly for mouse events, such as Event.MOUSE_DOWN.

```
public int key;
```

This is the key that was pressed or released (if this was a keyboard event). It will be the actual character value of the key if a normal key was pressed (in which case the *id* field will be Event.KEY_DOWN or Event.KEY_UP). It will be one of the special key codes listed above if a special key was pressed (in which case the *id* field will be Event.KEY_ACTION or Event.KEY_ACTION_RELEASE).

```
public int modifiers;
```

This will be one of the modifiers listed above, such as Event.SHIFT_MASK. The modifiers which indicate the modifying keys that were pressed at the time of the event, and will be or'ed together to create this integer.

```
public int clickCount;
```

This will represent the number of consecutive mouse clicks. If you get an Event.MOUSE_DOWN event, this can be used to determine if it was a double- or single-click. (It will be one in the former case, or two in the latter.)

```
public Object arg;
```

This is an additional argument which can be connected with the event. None of the standard Java events uses this field, but you can use it if you choose to create your own events.

```
public Event(Object target, long when, int id, int x, int y, int key, int modifiers,
Object arg);
public Event(Object target, long when, int id, int x, int y, int key, int modifiers);
public Event(Object target, int id, Object arg);
```

Although you wouldn't normally create Event objects, you might do so if you wanted to handle your own type of event. In that case, you would use one of these constructors.

```
public boolean shiftDown();
public boolean controlDown();
public boolean metaDown();
```

These methods tell you whether or not the <SHIFT>, <CONTROL>, or <META> keys were down at the time of the event. The <META> key isn't available on PC keyboards, but is available on keyboards for other platforms, such as the Macintosh.

```
public String toString();
```

This will convert the GridBagLayout object to a String. This can be helpful in debugging a program, especially if the String is then passed to System.out.println.

Exceptions

Listed below are all the standard Java exceptions. The runtime exceptions are not listed here—they are listed under the RuntimeExceptions heading.

You can create your own exceptions by sub-classing them to the Exception or RuntimeException classes.

Remember that you must handle the exception if you call a method which throws one of these. On the other hand, if a method throws a RuntimeException, you may handle it or not—as you wish.

```
AWTException
ClassNotFoundException
CloneNotSupportedException
```

```
EOFException
FileNotFoundException
IllegalAccessException
InstantiationException
InterruptedException
InterruptedIOException
IOException
NoSuchMethodException
MalformedURLException
ProtocolException
SocketException
UnknownHostException
UnknownServiceException
UTFDataFormatException
```

File (io)

Don't be fooled by the name of this class—it really deals with names, not files. Those names can apply to either files or directories.

The class does not allow you to create or access files, but it allows other functions such as renaming or deleting them.

```
public static final String separator;
public static final char separatorChar;
public static final String pathSeparator;
public static final char pathSeparatorChar;
```

117

These constants describe the separator that is used to divide directory names within a pathname, and the separator that is used to divide pathnames within a list of pathnames.

```
public File(String path);
public File(String path, String name);
public File(File dir, String name);
```

These methods let you create an object of the File class. There need not be a file or directory by the name you specified.

```
public String getName();
public String getPath();
```

These methods return the name of the item, and the path (excluding the name) of the item.

```
public String getParent();
```

This method returns the name of the directory in which the item (either a file or directory) described by the File object resides.

```
public boolean exists();
```

This method returns true if the item described by the File object exists.

```
public boolean canWrite();
public boolean canRead();
public boolean isFile();
public boolean isDirectory();
public native boolean isAbsolute();
```

These methods provide information about the item. The first two indicate whether or not you are allowed read and write access to the item. The next two indicate whether the item is a file or a directory. The last method indicates whether the name provided to the constructor was a complete pathname (rather than a partial, relative pathname). The first four methods will all return false if the item doesn't exist.

```
public long lastModified();
```

This method returns information about when the file was last modified. The value returned cannot be used to create a Date object, or otherwise be interpreted as a real time and date. It can, however, be compared to the value returned for other files. A larger value always indicates a later time and date.

The results of this method are undefined if the file doesn't exist, or if the File object represents a directory.

```
public long length();
```

118

This method returns the number of bytes in the file. The results are undefined if the file doesn't exist, or if the File object represents a directory.

```
public boolean mkdir();
public boolean mkdirs();
```

The first method assumes that the File object represents a directory, and that the directory in which it resides exists. It will try to create the directory, and will return true if it is successful.

The second method also assumes that the File object represents a directory, but it doesn't assume that it resides in an existing directory. It will create any directories on the path which do not exist. It returns true if it is successful.

```
public boolean renameTo(File dest);
```

This method renames the file or directory to the name given by dest. It returns true if successful.

```
public String[] list();
public String[] list(FilenameFilter filter);
```

These methods assume that the item described by the File object is a directory. The methods return an array of String objects, each of which is one of the items (either a file or a directory) in the directory.

```
public boolean delete();
```

This method will delete the file or directory. It returns true if the deletion is successful.

```
public boolean equals(Object obj);
```

This returns true if the obj is a File object, and if the pathnames are the same. (Note that one of the pathnames might be absolute, and the other relative, and still describe the same item. In this case, the two objects will be considered unequal.)

```
public String toString();
```

This will convert the File object to a String. This can be helpful in debugging a program, especially if the String is then passed to System.out.println.

FileDescriptor (io)

An object of this class represents a physical file which is currently open. It is similar to a file handle used in many Windows environments. It is rarely useful in Java, since you normally access a file through streams, without directly using one of these objects. You cannot create these objects on your own, but can obtain them from other methods (such as the *getFD* methods in the FileInputStream, FileOutputStream, and RandomAccessFile classes, or *getFileDescriptor* in the SocketImpl class).

FileDialog (AWT)

This class allows you to display a file selection dialog. This lets the user select an existing file to be opened or specify the name of a file to be created.

```
public static final int LOAD;
public static final int SAVE;
```

These are used for the *mode* parameter to the constructor. LOAD causes an open dialog, and SAVE causes a save dialog.

```
public FileDialog(Frame parent, String title);
public FileDialog(Frame parent, String title, int mode);
```

These constructors will create a FileDialog object. After creating the object, you need to call the *show* method for the object to cause the dialog to be executed.

```
public int getMode();
```

This returns the *mode* parameter specified in the constructor.

```
public String getDirectory();
public String getFile();
```

Use these methods after the dialog has been run (with the *show* method). They let you get the directory and file selected by the user.

```
public void setFile(String file);
public void setDirectory(String dir);
```

Use these methods before starting the dialog (with the *show* method). They let you specify the starting filename and directory to use in the dialog box.

```
public void setFilenameFilter(FilenameFilter filter);
public FilenameFilter getFilenameFilter();
```

Much of the time, you will want the dialog box to show all the files in a directory. But, you sometimes want to show just certain types of files. If you want to limit the files, you can do so by creating a sub-class of FilenameFilter that will indicate which files are to be included, and which are not. You should create an object of this sub-class, and pass it to setFilenameFilter for it to take effect.

FileInputStream (io)

This is the kind of InputStream that is connected to a file. (As such, it's probably the most common kind of InputStream.)

Although you can read data directly from this kind of InputStream, it is more common to use the FileInputStream object as the parameter to the constructor for a BufferedInputStream or DataInputStream object. (The BufferedInputStream object may, in turn, be used in the constructor for a DataInputStream object.) This gives you the ability to use the more complete set of methods in the DataInputStream class.

```
public FileInputStream(String name) throws FileNotFoundException;
public FileInputStream(File file) throws FileNotFoundException;
public FileInputStream(FileDescriptor fdObj);
```

These constructors allow you to create a FileInputStream object. The most common form is the first one, which takes a name as the parameter. The name can be a simple filename, a partial pathname, or a complete pathname.

You can also use a File or FileDescriptor object in the constructor. (Using a FileDescriptor would be unusual.)

```
public native int read() throws IOException;
public int read(byte b[]) throws IOException;
public int read(byte b[], int offset, int len) throws IOException;
```

These methods let you read data from the stream. The first reads a single character. The second reads up to *b.length* bytes into array *b*. The third reads up to *len* bytes into array *b* starting at index offset. The second and third methods will return the number of bytes actually read. All three will return -1 if the end of the stream is encountered before any bytes can be read.

```
public native long skip(long n) throws IOException;
```

This method skips past the next *n* bytes. It returns the actual number of bytes skipped.

```
public native int available() throws IOException;
```

This method returns the number of bytes which can be obtained from the stream without reading more data from the disk.

```
public native void close() throws IOException;
```

This method closes the file.

```
public final FileDescriptor getFD() throws IOException;
```

This method returns a FileDescriptor object for the stream. This is rarely useful.

FilenameFilter (io)

This is an interface which describes a single method: the *accept* method. This method is used to indicate whether or not a filename should pass through a filter. It is used to determine which files should be displayed by a FileDialog object. (Files which pass through the filter are displayed; those which don't are not.)

```
boolean accept(File dir, String name);
```

This method should return true if the file passes the filter (and should be used by the method that called it), or false if it doesn't pass (and thus shouldn't be used).

FileOutputStream (io)

This is the kind of OutputStream that is connected to a file. (As such, it's probably the most common kind of OutputStream.)

Although you can write data directly to this kind of OutputStream, it is more common to use the FileOutputStream object as the parameter to the constructor for a BufferedOutputStream or DataOutputStream object. (The BufferedOutputStream object may, in turn, be used in the constructor for a DataOutputStream object.) This gives you the ability to use the more complete set of methods in the DataOutputStream class.

```
public FileOutputStream(String name) throws IOException;
public FileOutputStream(File file) throws IOException;
public FileOutputStream(FileDescriptor fdObj);
```

These constructors let you create objects of the FileOutputStream class.

The most common form is the first one, which takes a *name* as the parameter. The name can be a simple filename, a partial pathname, or a complete pathname.

You can also use a File or FileDescriptor object in the constructor. (Using a FileDescriptor would be unusual.)

```
public native void write(int b) throws IOException;
public void write(byte b[]) throws IOException;
public void write(byte b[], int off, int len) throws IOException;
```

These methods write data to the stream. The first form writes a single byte of data. The second form writes all the bytes in the array. The third form writes *len* bytes starting at index offset in the array.

```
public native void close() throws IOException;
```

This method closes the file.

```
public final FileDescriptor getFD()  throws IOException;
```

This obtains a FileDescriptor object for the file. Such an object is rarely useful.

```
public void flush() throws IOException;
```

This method flushes any buffers used by the stream, writing all the temporary data to the file.

FilteredImageSource (AWT.Image)

This class is a type of ImageProducer. It takes an image, filters it using an ImageFilter, and passes the result on. This class would not be used directly in a program which is simply displaying an image; like most of the classes in AWT.Image, it is used only for the unusual case in which image manipulation is to be done.

```
public FilteredImageSource(ImageProducer orig, ImageFilter imgf);
public synchronized void addConsumer(ImageConsumer ic);
public synchronized boolean isConsumer(ImageConsumer ic);
public synchronized void removeConsumer(ImageConsumer ic);
public void startProduction(ImageConsumer ic);
public void requestTopDownLeftRightResend(ImageConsumer ic);
```

FilterInputStream (io)

This class is the super-class of other filtering classes, such as BufferedInputStream. You would never create an object of this class directly, but you might sub-class it if you wanted to provide your own method of filtering a stream. In this case, you would override at least the *read* methods, and you probably should override all the methods in the class.

```
protected FilterInputStream(InputStream in);
```

This constructor lets you create objects of this class, although you cannot do so directly. Only your sub-class will be able to call this constructor.

```
public int read() throws IOException;
public int read(byte b[]) throws IOException;
public int read(byte b[], int off, int len) throws IOException;
```

These methods let you read bytes from the stream. The first will return a single byte obtained from the stream. The second will read up to *b.length* bytes into *b*. The third will read up to *len* bytes into *b* beginning at index off. The second and third methods will return the number of bytes actually read from the stream. All three methods will return -1 if the end of the stream is reached.

```
public long skip(long n) throws IOException;
```

This method will skip past the next *n* bytes in the stream. It returns the actual number of bytes skipped.

```
public int available() throws IOException;
```

This method returns the number of bytes which can be obtained from the input stream without having to perform a disk or network read operation.

```
public void close() throws IOException;
```

This method closes the stream.

```
public synchronized void mark(int readlimit);
public synchronized void reset() throws IOException;
```

The *mark* method will mark the current location in the stream. You can later return to that location by calling *reset*. The *readlimit* is the maximum number of bytes you can read after calling *mark* and before calling *reset*. If you read more than *readlimit* bytes, you will no longer be able to call *reset*.

```
public boolean markSupported();
```

This method returns true if the *mark* and *reset* methods are supported.

FilterOutputStream (io)

This class is the super-class of other filtering classes, such as BufferedOutputStream. You would never create an object of this class directly, but you might sub-class it if you wanted to provide your own method of filtering a stream. In this case, you would override at least the *write* methods, and you probably should override all the methods in the class.

```
public FilterOutputStream(OutputStream out);
```

This method allows you to create objects of this class, although you would not do that directly. Only your sub-class would call this constructor.

```
public void write(int b) throws IOException;
public void write(byte b[]) throws IOException;
public void write(byte b[], int off, int len) throws IOException;
```

123

These methods let you write bytes to the stream. The first method writes a single byte. The second method writes *b.length* bytes from array *b*. The third method writes *len* bytes starting from index off in array *b*.

```
public void flush() throws IOException;
```

This method will flush any buffers the class uses—that is, it will send on to the output stream any data it has been holding temporarily.

```
public void close() throws IOException;
```

This method closes the stream.

Float (lang)

Objects of this class are immutable. That means they are assigned a value when they are created, and that value cannot be changed later. If you want the object to have a different value, you must create a new object with that new value.

```
public static final float POSITIVE_INFINITY;
public static final float NEGATIVE_INFINITY;
public static final float NaN;
public static final float MAX_VALUE;
public static final float MIN_VALUE;
```

IEEE specs allow a floating point number to have a few special values. Those values are listed here, and can be used to compare against *double* variables.

```
public Double(double value);
public Double(float value);
public Double(String s) throws NumberFormatException;
```

These constructors allow you to create a *Double*.

```
public static native String toString(float d);
```

This converts a *double* to a String.

```
static public boolean isNaN(float v);
static public boolean isInfinite(float v);
```

These methods return true if the value is not a number or is infinite.

```
public boolean isNaN();
public boolean isInfinite();
```

These methods return true if the object is not a number or is infinite.

```
public String toString();
public int intValue();
public long longValue();
public float floatValue();
public double doubleValue();
```

This converts the *Double* to other types.

```
public boolean equals(Object obj);
```

This returns true if the obj is a *Double*, and if it has the same numeric value.

```
public static native int floatToIntBits(double value);
public static native float intBitsToFloat(long bits);
```

These allow you to copy a sequence of bits that are stored in a *long* to a location that is treated as a *double*, and vice versa. No conversion is performed here; the bits are simply copied from one location to another and assumed to be in the proper format.

FlowLayout (AWT)

```
public static final int LEFT;
public static final int CENTER
public static final int RIGHT;
```

These constants are used in calls to the constructor.

```
public FlowLayout();
public FlowLayout(int align);
public FlowLayout(int align, int hgap, int vgap);
```

The *align* parameter determines how the Components are positioned within the Container if there is extra space. The default alignment is CENTER.

By default, the Components will have a small gap between them; if you wish to specify how large this gap should be, you can use the *hgap* and *vgap* parameters.

```
public void addLayoutComponent(String name, Component comp);
public void removeLayoutComponent(Component comp);
public void layoutContainer(Container target);
```

Although these are public methods, you shouldn't call them. Instead, you should use the *add* method of the Container class to add components to the layout.

```
public Dimension minimumLayoutSize(Container target);
public Dimension preferredLayoutSize(Container target);
```

These methods let you find out how much space the components would take if laid out in the given Container. You should call the *pack* method for the Container before calling either of these methods.

```
public String toString();
```

This will convert the FlowLayout object to a String. This can be helpful in debugging a program, especially if the String is then passed to System.out.println.

Font (AWT)

```
public static final int PLAIN;
public static final int BOLD;
public static final int ITALIC;
```

These values can be used for the *style* parameter in the constructor.

```
public Font(String name, int style, int size);
```

This constructor allows you to create Font objects.

The *name* parameter is the Java name for a font, which is often different from the name used for the font on the native system. The available Java names are Helvetica, TimesRoman, Courier, Dialog, DialogInput, and ZapfDingbats.

The size specifies the size of the font. Be careful because in some environments this is the point size of the font, and in others it is the pixel height of the font.

```
public String getFamily();
public String getName();
```

These methods return the name of the font. The first method returns the name used on the platform that is running the program, and the second returns the name used by Java.

```
public int getStyle();
public int getSize();
public boolean isPlain();
public boolean isBold();
public boolean isItalic();
```

These methods allow you to determine the size and style of the font.

```
public String toString();
```

This will convert the Font object to a String. This can be helpful in debugging a program, especially if the String is then passed to System.out.println.

FontMetrics (AWT)

This class provides information about a font. You would normally create an object of this class by using the *getFontMetrics* method in the Graphics or Component classes. (Because it is in the Component class, you can use the method for Frame objects, which is the most common place you will be drawing with fonts.)

```
public Font getFont();
```

This method returns the font for which the object was created.

```
public int getLeading();
public int getAscent();
public int getDescent();
public int getHeight();
public int getMaxAscent();
public int getMaxDescent();
public int getMaxAdvance();
```

These methods give you information about the amount of space the font takes when displayed. The leading is the amount of space that should be left between lines of text. The ascent and descent are the amount of space that should be left above and below the baseline for each line of text. The height is the sum of the ascent, descent, and leading. The maximum ascent and maximum descent are the largest amount of ascent and descent actually used by any of the characters in the font.

126

```
public int charWidth(int ch);
public int charWidth(char ch);
public int stringWidth(String str);
public int charsWidth(char data[], int off, int len);
public int bytesWidth(byte data[], int off, int len);
public int[] getWidths();
```

These methods provide information about the width of text written with the font. The *charWidth* methods return the width of a single character. The *stringWidth* method returns the width of a string of characters. The *charsWidth* and *bytesWidth* methods return the total width of a series of characters that are stored in an array. The characters used within the array are the *len* characters beginning with index off within the array. The *getWidths* method returns an array with 256 elements. Each element returns the width for one character (i.e., the first element of the array returns the width of the character with an ASCII value of zero, the second for an ASCII value of one, etc.).

```
public String toString();
```

This will convert the FontMetric object to a String. This can be helpful in debugging a program, especially if the String is then passed to System.out.println.

Frame

Frame is a sub-class of Container, Window, and Component, so you can use methods from any of those classes, as well as those listed below, to control a Frame object.

```
public static final int DEFAULT_CURSOR;
public static final int CROSSHAIR_CURSOR;
public static final int TEXT_CURSOR;
public static final int WAIT_CURSOR;
public static final int SW_RESIZE_CURSOR;
public static final int SE_RESIZE_CURSOR;
public static final int NW_RESIZE_CURSOR;
public static final int NE_RESIZE_CURSOR;
public static final int N_RESIZE_CURSOR;
public static final int S_RESIZE_CURSOR;
public static final int W_RESIZE_CURSOR;
public static final int E_RESIZE_CURSOR;
public static final int HAND_CURSOR;
public static final int MOVE_CURSOR;
```

These values can be used in calls to getCursor and setCursorType.

```
public Frame();
public Frame(String title);
```

These are the constructors for Frame objects. The first version will cause the frame to be untitled, which usually means that untitled will appear at the top of the frame.

```
public String getTitle();
public void setTitle(String title);
```

These methods let you set and get the title that appears at the top of the frame.

```
public Image getIconImage();
public void setIconImage(Image image);
```

These methods let you get and set the image used to identify the frame when it is minimized (i.e., when it is reduced to an icon at the bottom of the screen). By default, the icon for a Java program is an image of the Java coffee cup.

```
public MenuBar getMenuBar();
public synchronized void setMenuBar(MenuBar mb);
```

These methods let you set and get the menu bar that will appear on the frame. (The *mb* parameter cannot be null; to remove the menu bar, use *remove*.)

```
public synchronized void remove(MenuComponent m);
```

This method lets you remove a menu, menu item, or menu bar from the frame's menu.

```
public synchronized void dispose();
```

This method should be used to remove the frame from the screen.

```
public boolean isResizable();
public void setResizable(boolean resizable);
```

127

These methods let you get or set the resizable option. This option controls whether or not the user is allowed to change the size of the frame.

```
public void setCursor(int cursorType);
public int getCursorType();
```

These methods let you get and set the cursor that will be displayed whenever the mouse is positioned over the frame. You can use any of the cursor constants listed above.

Graphics (AWT)

This is one of the key classes in Java. It allows you to draw on the screen. Although you can create objects of the Graphics class, you normally don't—instead, you simply use the Graphics object sent to the update or paint methods in the Component class. (You will often override those methods in sub-classes of Frame or Canvas.)

The methods in this class that begin with the word "draw" will draw an outline of the specified shape. For example, *drawRect* draws four lines that make a rectangular shape. The methods that begin with the word "fill" will draw an area of color of the specified shape. For example, *fillRect* will draw a rectangularly-shaped area of color.

All drawing, whether of text or of some graphic shape, will always be done in just one color, and that color can be selected with the *setColor* method.

```
public Graphics create();
public Graphics create(int x, int y, int width, int height);
```

These methods let you create new Graphics objects. (You can't create one from scratch with the *new* operator. Instead, you use these methods to create a copy of an existing object.) The first method creates an exact copy of the Graphics object, while the second one creates a new object that has the given location and size.

```
public void translate(int x, int y);
```

This method makes the given location the new origin for the Graphics object. All subsequent calls to *Graphics* methods will use the new origin for positioning.

```
public Color getColor();
public void setColor(Color c);
```

These methods let you get and set the color to be used for subsequent drawing.

```
public void setPaintMode();
public void setXORMode(Color c1);
```

These methods let you control the way subsequent drawing will be done. Calling *setPaintMode* says that items drawn will overwrite previous items. (That is the default mode.) Calling *setXORMode* means that pixels on the screen which are *cl* will be changed to the current color, and pixels which are the current color will become *cl*. (The current color is the one set by *setColor*.)

```
public Font getFont();
public void setFont(Font font);
```

These methods let you set and get the font to be used for subsequent drawing of text.

```
public FontMetrics getFontMetrics();
public FontMetrics getFontMetrics(Font f);
```

These methods let you obtain a FontMetrics object. This object provides useful information about the size of the characters drawn in the font. The first version of *getFontMetrics* gets an object for the font selected by a previous call to *setFont*. The second version of *getFontMetrics* uses font *f*.

```
public Rectangle getClipRect();
public void clipRect(int x, int y, int width, int height);
```

These methods let you get and set the clipping rectangle. The clipping rectangle is a rectangular area within which drawing will take place. Any drawing done outside the rectangle is ignored. By default, the clipping rectangle is the same size as the Container (such as the Frame) in which drawing is being done. That means drawing is only limited to the Container. You can make the rectangle smaller if you wish.

```
public void drawLine(int x1, int y1, int x2, int y2);
```

This method draws a line between the two positions.

```
public void fillRect(int x, int y, int width, int height);
public void drawRect(int x, int y, int width, int height);
public void clearRect(int x, int y, int width, int height);
```

These methods let you fill, draw, or clear a rectangle.

```
public void drawRoundRect(int x, int y, int width, int height, int arcWidth, ⇐
int arcHeight);
public void fillRoundRect(int x, int y, int width, int height, int arcWidth, ⇐
int arcHeight);
```

These methods let you fill and draw rectangles that have rounded corners. The *arcHeight* and *arcWidth* parameters specify the height and width of each of the ovals used to round the corners.

```
public void draw3DRect(int x, int y, int width, int height, boolean raised);
public void fill3DRect(int x, int y, int width, int height, boolean raised);
```

These methods let you draw and fill rctangles that have a three-dimensional appearance. The *raised* parameter will be true if the rectangle should appear higher than the surrounding area, or false if it should appear lower.

```
public void drawOval(int x, int y, int width, int height);
public void fillOval(int x, int y, int width, int height);
```

These methods let you fill or draw an oval.

```
public void drawArc(int x, int y, int width, int height, int startAngle, int arcAngle);
public void fillArc(int x, int y, int width, int height, int startAngle, int arcAngle);
```

These methods let you fill or draw an arc (i.e., part of an oval). The arc will begin at the location specified by *startAngle*. The *startAngle* is measured in degrees, and moves counter-clockwise from the right-most point on the oval (the point that would be 3:00 if the oval were a clock face). The arc will then continue counter-clockwise by *arcAngle* degrees.

```
public void drawPolygon(int xPoints[], int yPoints[], int nPoints);
public void drawPolygon(Polygon p);
public abstract void fillPolygon(int xPoints[], int yPoints[], int nPoints);
public void fillPolygon(Polygon p);
```

These methods let you draw or fill a polygon. To specify the polygon, you can either use a Polygon object, or you can use an array of points. Each point represents one corner of the polygon.

```
public void drawString(String str, int x, int y);
public void drawChars(char data[], int offset, int length, int x, int y);
public void drawBytes(byte data[], int offset, int length, int x, int y);
```

These methods allow you to draw text. The font can be specified with the *setFont* method.

```
public boolean drawImage(Image img, int x, int y, ImageObserver observer);

public abstract boolean drawImage(Image img, int x, int y, int width, int height,
ImageObserver observer);
public boolean drawImage(Image img, int x, int y, Color bgcolor, ImageObserver observer);
public boolean drawImage(Image img, int x, int y, int width, int height, Color bgcolor,⇐
ImageObserver observer);
```

These methods let you draw an image. The contents of the image are contained in an Image object, which most commonly would be obtained from the *getImage* method in the Applet class.

You should normally pass the Java keyword *this* for the *observer* parameter. That will cause the *paint* method for your applet to be called again automatically when more of the image has been obtained from the network.

```
public void dispose();
public String toString();
```

This will convert the Graphics object to a String. This can be helpful in debugging a program, especially if the String is then passed to System.out.println.

GridBagConstraints (AWT)

Objects of this class are used to tell a GridBagLayout object how a given component is to be placed in a container. (Because of the complexity of the GridBagLayout class, there are quite a few options for how a component is placed in the container. This object lets you control all those options.)

```
public static final int RELATIVE;
```

This can be used in the *gridx* or *gridy* field variables.

```
public static final int REMAINDER;
```

This can be used in the *gridheight* or *gridwidth* field variables.

```
public static final int NONE;
public static final int BOTH;
public static final int HORIZONTAL;
public static final int VERTICAL;
```

These are used in the *fill* field variable.

```
public static final int CENTER;
public static final int NORTH;
public static final int NORTHEAST;
public static final int EAST;
public static final int SOUTHEAST;
public static final int SOUTH;
public static final int SOUTHWEST;
public static final int WEST;
public static final int NORTHWEST;
```

These are used in the *anchor* field variable.

```
public int gridx, gridy;
```

These indicate the row (*gridx*) and column (*gridy*) the Component should be in. The first row or column is zero, the second is one, and so forth.

They can be set to GridBagConstraints.RELATIVE to indicate that it should be placed immediately following the last Component that was added.

```
public int gridwidth, gridheight;
```

131

These values specify the number of rows and columns the Component spans. For example, setting gridwidth to 2 means the Component spans two columns.

They can be set to GridBagConstraints.REMAINDER to indicate that the Component should take up the rest of the row.

```
public double weightx, weighty;
```

These assign weights to the rows and columns the Component occupies. The weights will effect the amount of extra space each Component receives. Extra space is space left over after the basic layout has been done. (It is often best to set these values to 1 for each of your Components.)

```
public int anchor;
```

This indicates how the Component should be positioned within the row(s) and column(s) it occupies. It can be GridBagConstraint.CENTER or any of the direction constants.

```
public int fill;
```

This controls how the Component grows into the space allocated for it. It can be GridBagConstraint.NONE, GridBagConstraint.BOTH, GridBagConstraint.HORIZONTAL, or GridBagConstraint.VERTICAL. For example, if you pick HORIZONTAL, the Component will grow in width, but will not grow in height.

```
public Insets insets;
```

This controls the extra space, if any, that should be placed around the outside of the Component.

GridBagLayout (AWT)

This class allows you to create layout manager objects that put objects in a grid. Unlike the GridLayout class, the rows and columns in this class can vary in size. Also, objects can span more than one row or column.

```
public int columnWidths[];
public int rowHeights[];
public double columnWeights[];
public double rowWeights[];
```

These public arrays give you the characteristics of the rows and columns in the grid. You should call *pack* before using columnWidths[] or rowHeights[].

```
public GridBagLayout();
```

This constructor lets you create GridBagLayout objects.

```
public void setConstraints(Component comp, GridBagConstraints constraints);
public GridBagConstraints getConstraints(Component comp);
```

132

Use *setConstraints* to set the values the layout manager will use to position a given Component in the Container. It is a critical method for this class, and one you will need to use for every Component you put in the Container. To use it, you will need to create a GridBagConstraints object, and set all of its field variables. Then, call *setConstraints* to pass that information to the layout manager. After calling *setConstraints*, you can re-use the same GridBagConstraints object, since the layout manager keeps a copy of the object for its own use.

You can use *getConstraints* to get a copy of the GridBagConstraints object later, if you wish.

```
public Point getLayoutOrigin();
```

This method returns the coordinates of the upper left-hand corner of the grid.

```
public int [][] getLayoutDimensions();
```

This method returns a two-dimensional array that gives the width of each column and the height of each row. The first dimension of the array should be zero to indicate column, and one to indicate row. The second dimension should be the row or column number.

```
public double [][] getLayoutWeights();
```

This array returns the weight of each row and column. The subscripts for the two-dimension array work just as they do for getLayoutDimensions, above.

```
public Point location(int x, int y);
```

This method returns the row and column of the grid which contains a given *x* and *y* coordinate.

```
public void addLayoutComponent(String name, Component comp);
public void removeLayoutComponent(Component comp);
public void layoutContainer(Container target);
```

Although these are public methods, you shouldn't call them. Instead, you should use the *add* method of the Container class to add components to the layout.

```
public Dimension minimumLayoutSize(Container target);
public Dimension preferredLayoutSize(Container target);
```

These methods let you find out how much space the components would take if laid out in the given Container. You should call the *pack* method for the Container before calling either of these methods.

```
public String toString();
```

This will convert the GridBagLayout object to a String. This can be helpful in debugging a program, especially if the String is then passed to System.out.println.

GridLayout (AWT)

This kind of LayoutManager lets you place components in rows and columns. All rows are the same height, and all columns are the same width. Each component can occupy only one row and one column. (Don't get this class confused with its much more complicated brother, GridBagLayout.)

```
public GridLayout(int rows, int cols);
public GridLayout(int rows, int cols, int hgap, int vgap);
```

These constructors setup a grid which is *rows* high and *cols* wide. Each row is the same height, and each column is the same width. The *hgap* and *vgap* parameters indicate the amount of empty space to be left between each row and column.

```
public void addLayoutComponent(String name, Component comp);
public void removeLayoutComponent(Component comp);
public void layoutContainer(Container target);
```

Although these are public methods, you shouldn't call them. Instead, you should use the *add* method of the Container class to add components to the layout.

```
public Dimension minimumLayoutSize(Container target);
public Dimension preferredLayoutSize(Container target);
```

These methods let you find out how much space the components would take if laid out in the given Container. You should call the *pack* method for the Container before calling either of these methods.

```
public String toString();
```

This will convert the GridLayout object to a String. This can be helpful in debugging a program, especially if the String is then passed to System.out.println.

Hashtable (util)

This class helps you build an index of objects. Each object placed in the index must have a unique key value. Once the index is built, you can supply a key value to the table, and it will return the object with that key.

In order for objects of a given class to be stored in a hashtable, the class must provide three features. The first is that each object in the class must have a unique key. That key is often made up of one or more of the field variables of that class, but it doesn't have to be. All that is required is that you be able to supply the key when you add the object to the table.

The second thing which must be supplied by a class is an *equals* method. This method should follow the rules laid out for *equals* in the Object class. This method allows two objects to be compared to see if they have the same contents.

The final thing which must be supplied by a class is a *hashcode* method. This method returns an integer which identifies the object. The integer doesn't have to uniquely identify the object, but the more uniquely it identifies objects the more effeciently the hashtable will work. The *hashtable* method should follow the rules for it laid out in the Object class.

```
public Hashtable(int initialCapacity, float loadFactor);
public Hashtable(int initialCapacity);
public Hashtable();
```

134

These constructors let you create objects of the Hashtable class. The initialCapacity parameter indicates the number of spaces for objects to be allocated in the table. You need not worry too much about this capacity, since the table will grow as needed when you add new objects to it. The loadFactor is a value between zero and one. It indicates how full the table should get before making the table larger. For example, if you passed .75 for this value, the table would grow when it became 75 percent full. (For reasons of efficiency, you don't want the table to become completely full.)

If you don't provide either initialCapacity or loadFactor, default values will be used.

```
public int size();
```

This method returns the number of objects currently stored in the table.

```
public boolean isEmpty();
```

This will be true if there are not currently any objects in the table.

```
public synchronized Enumeration keys();
public synchronized Enumeration elements();
```

These methods each return an Enumeration object. This object can be used to retrieve each of the objects in the table, one at a time. The *keys* method will allow you to retrieve the key for each object, and the *elements* method will allow you to retrieve each object itself.

```
public synchronized boolean contains(Object value);
public synchronized boolean containsKey(Object key);
```

These methods return true if the table contains a given object, or an object with the given key.

```
public synchronized Object get(Object key);
```

This method searches the table for an object with the given key. If it finds one, it will return it. If it doesn't, it will return null.

```
public synchronized Object put(Object key, Object value);
public synchronized Object remove(Object key);
```

These methods let you add and remove objects from the table.

```
public synchronized void clear();
```

This method removes all the objects from the table.

```
public synchronized Object clone();
```

This method creates a complete copy of the Hashtable object. This new table will contain the same objects that the old one did. (It doesn't contain copies of those objects, but rather the same objects.)

```
public String toString();
```

This will convert the Hashtable object to a String. For many classes, this can be helpful in debugging a program, especially if the String is then passed to System.out.println. For Hashtable, the string produced can be quite lengthy, and thus may not be of as much value.

135

Image (AWT)

Objects of this class represent an image which can be drawn on the screen. These images are most commonly obtained by the *getImage* method in the Applet class, which converts a .gif file into an Image object.

Although objects of this class can be useful, the methods provided by the class rarely are. They are primarily useful for internal Java code.

```
public int getWidth(ImageObserver observer);
public int getHeight(ImageObserver observer);
```

These methods return the height and width of the image. This information may not be known, in which case -1 is returned.

```
public ImageProducer getSource();
```

This obtains the source of the image, which is an ImageProducer object.

```
public Graphics getGraphics();
```

If the image is being used for off-screen drawing, this method can obtain a Graphics object for the drawing.

ImageConsumer (AWT.Image)

This interface describes the methods an ImageProducer object uses to pass information to an entity which will be using that image. That information allows the consumer to draw and otherwise handle the image. This interface would not be used directly in a program which is simply displaying an image; like most of the classes in AWT.Image, it is used only for the unusual case in which image manipulation is to be done.

```
void setDimensions(int width, int height);
void setProperties(Hashtable props);
void setColorModel(ColorModel model);
void setHints(int hintflags);
int RANDOMPIXELORDER;
int TOPDOWNLEFTRIGHT;
int COMPLETESCANLINES;
int SINGLEPASS;
int SINGLEFRAME;
void setPixels(int x, int y, int w, int h, ColorModel model, byte pixels[], int off, ⇐
int scansize);
void setPixels(int x, int y, int w, int h, ColorModel model, int pixels[], int off, int
scansize);
void imageComplete(int status);
int IMAGEERROR;
int SINGLEFRAMEDONE;
int STATICIMAGEDONE;
int IMAGEABORTED;
```

136

ImageFilter (AWT.Image)

This class can filter an image. It does this by taking the output from an ImageProducer and altering it before delivering it to the ultimate ImageConsumer. The class itself does no filtering, but sub-classes can perform filtering. This class would not be used directly in a program which is simply displaying an image; like most of the classes in AWT.Image, it is used only for the unusual case in which image manipulation is to be done.

```
public ImageFilter getFilterInstance(ImageConsumer ic);
public void setDimensions(int width, int height);
public void setProperties(Hashtable props);
public void setColorModel(ColorModel model);
public void setHints(int hints);
public void setPixels(int x, int y, int w, int h, ColorModel model, byte pixels[], ⇐
int off, int scansize);
public void setPixels(int x, int y, int w, int h, ColorModel model, int pixels[], ⇐
int off, int scansize);
public void imageComplete(int status);
public void resendTopDownLeftRight(ImageProducer ip);
```

ImageObserver (AWT.Image)

This interface describes entities which want to observe the progress of an image as it is being produced. All sub-classes of the Component class implement this interface since they can all draw images in their area of the screen. This class would not be used directly in a program which is simply displaying an image; like most of the classes in AWT.Image, it is used only for the unusual case in which image manipulation is to be done.

```
public boolean imageUpdate(Image img, int infoflags, int x, int y, int width, ⇐
int height);
public static final int WIDTH;
public static final int HEIGHT;
public static final int PROPERTIES;
public static final int SOMEBITS;
public static final int FRAMEBITS;
public static final int ALLBITS;
public static final int ERROR;
public static final int ABORT;
```

ImageProducer (AWT.Image)

This class embodies objects which produce images. Often, for example, an image resides on the Internet in the form of a .gif file. In that case, an ImageProducer object would read the data from the .gif file and convert it to the proper Image format. Each ImageProducer object has an ImageConsumer object (or perhaps several) to which it sends the converted data. This class would not be used directly in a program which is simply displaying an image; like most of the classes in AWT.Image, it is used only for the unusual case in which image manipulation is to be done.

```
public void addConsumer(ImageConsumer ic);
public boolean isConsumer(ImageConsumer ic);
public void removeConsumer(ImageConsumer ic);
public void startProduction(ImageConsumer ic);
public void requestTopDownLeftRightResend(ImageConsumer ic);
```

IndexColorModel (AWT.Image)

This class describes a way of storing color in pixels in which each pixel contains the index to an array, and that array contains the red, green, and blue components of the color. This class would not be used directly in a program which is simply displaying an image; like most of the classes in AWT.Image, it is used only for the unusual case in which image manipulation is to be done.

```
public IndexColorModel(int bits, int size, byte r[], byte g[], byte b[]);
public IndexColorModel(int bits, int size, byte r[], byte g[], byte b[], int trans);
public IndexColorModel(int bits, int size, byte r[], byte g[], byte b[], byte a[]);
```

continued on next page

continued from previous page

```
public IndexColorModel(int bits, int size, byte cmap[], int start, boolean hasalpha);
public IndexColorModel(int bits, int size, byte cmap[], int start, boolean hasalpha, ⇐
int trans);
final public int getMapSize();
final public int getTransparentPixel();
final public void getReds(byte r[]);
final public void getGreens(byte g[]);
final public void getBlues(byte b[]);
final public void getAlphas(byte a[]);
final public int getRed(int pixel);
final public int getGreen(int pixel);
final public int getBlue(int pixel);
final public int getAlpha(int pixel);
final public int getRGB(int pixel);
```

InetAddress (net)

This class describes Internet addresses. It is used behind the scenes by other Java classes; you would only use it if you were performing low-level Internet communications.

```
public String getHostName();
public byte[] getAddress();
public boolean equals(Object obj);
public String toString();
public static synchronized InetAddress getByName(String host) throws UnknownHostException;
public static synchronized InetAddress getAllByName(String host)[] throws ⇐
UnknownHostException;
public static synchronized InetAddress getAllByName(String host)[] throws ⇐
UnknownHostException
public static InetAddress getLocalHost() throws UnknownHostException;
```

InputStream (io)

This is an abstract class which groups together all the forms of input streams: ByteArrayInputStream, FileInputStream, FilterInputStream, PipedInputStream, SequenceInputtream, and StringBufferInputStream. Those sub-classes override most of the methods of this class, so they are listed in the sub-classes rather than here.

Insets (AWT)

This simple class defines objects which identify the amount of margin to be left at the edge of something. For example, an object of this class can be obtained from the *insets* method in the Container class, and describes the margins to be left around the edge of the container.

```
public int top;
public int left;
public int bottom;
public int right;
```

These field variables indicate the amount of margin for each of the four sides of the area.

```
public Insets(int top, int left, int bottom, int right);
```

This constructor lets you create Insets objects.

```
public String toString();
```

This will convert the Insets object to a String. This can be helpful in debugging a program, especially if the String is then passed to System.out.println.

Integer (lang)

Objects of this class are immutable. That means they are assigned a value when they are created, and that value cannot be changed later. If you want the object to have a different value, you must create a new object with that new value.

Note that this class is spelled Integer, not Int.

```
public static final int MIN_VALUE;
public static final int MAX_VALUE;
```

These are the minimum and maximum values an *int* may have.

```
public Integer(int value);
public Integer(String s) throws NumberFormatException;
```

These constructors allow you to create an Integer object.

```
public static String toString(int i, int radix);
public static String toString(int i);
```

These convert the *int* to a String. The second form assumes a radix of 10.

```
public static int parseInt(String s, int radix) throws NumberFormatException;
public static int parseInt(String s) throws NumberFormatException;
public static Integer valueOf(String s, int radix) throws NumberFormatException;
public static Integer valueOf(String s) throws NumberFormatException;
```

These methods convert a String holding an integer value. The first two create an *int*, and the second two create an Integer. The forms without a *radix* parameter assume a radix of 10.

```
public int intValue();
public long longValue();
public float floatValue();
public double doubleValue();
public String toString();
```

These methods convert the Integer to other types.

```
public boolean equals(Object obj);
```

This returns *true* if *obj* is an *Integer* and it has the same numeric value.

Label (AWT)

A Label object represents text which is (normally) displayed in a dialog. It is like a control in many ways, but cannot be operated by the user and does not generate events.

Label is a sub-class of Component, so you can use any of the Component methods on a Label object.

```
public static final int LEFT;
public static final int CENTER;
public static final int RIGHT;
```

These literals are used with the constructor, the *getAlignment*, and the *setAlignment* methods.

```
public Label();
public Label(String label);
public Label(String label, int alignment);
```

These constructors allow you to create a Label object. The first is not very useful, since it creates an object with no text, unless you intend to set the text later with the *setLabel* method. The first and second constructors create a label which is left-justified. The third constructor can create a label with one of three kinds of justification: Label.LEFT, Label.CENTER, or Label.RIGHT.

```
public int getAlignment();
public void setAlignment(int alignment);
```

These methods allow you to get and set the alignment for the text. You can use Label.LEFT, Label.CENTER, or Label.RIGHT for the alignment.

```
public String getText();
public void setText(String label);
```

140

These methods let you get and set the text in the label.

LayoutManager (AWT)

This is an interface, not a class. If you want to write your own layout manager, you should write a class that implements this one.

```
void addLayoutComponent(String name, Component comp);
```

This method will be called once for each Component added to the Container. The *name* parameter is the one specified by the user in the *add* method of the Container class; it can be null.

```
void removeLayoutComponent(Component comp);
```

This method is called to remove a Component previously added with a call to addLayoutComponent.

```
Dimension preferredLayoutSize(Container parent);
```

This method should return the preferred size for the Container, which was previously calculated during the last call to layoutContainer.

```
Dimension minimumLayoutSize(Container parent);
```

This method should return the preferred size for the Container, which was previously calculated during the last call to layoutContainer.

```
void layoutContainer(Container parent);
```

This method will be called when the layout manager should calculate the layout for the current Components. As part of those calculations, the actual Component objects should be moved to the calculated positions.

LineNumberInputStream (io)

This is an ordinary input stream except that it provides one additional method, *getLineNumber,* which will tell you how many lines of text you have read so far.

```
public LineNumberInputStream(InputStream in);
```

This constructor lets you create an object of the LineNumberInputStream class.

```
public native int read() throws IOException;
public int read(byte b[]) throws IOException;
public int read(byte b[], int offset, int len) throws IOException;
```

These methods let you read data from the stream. The first reads and returns a single character. The second reads up to *b.length* bytes into array *b*. The third reads up to *len* bytes into array *b* starting at index offset. The second and third will return the number of bytes actually read. All three methods will return -1 if the end of the stream is encountered before any bytes can be read.

```
public void setLineNumber(int lineNumber);
public int getLineNumber();
```

These methods let you get and set the line number. (You wouldn't normally set it.) Calling *read* will automatically increase the line number if an end-of-line sequence is encountered. An end-of-line sequence is a '\r', or a '\n', or a '\n' followed by a '\r'.

```
public native long skip(long n) throws IOException;
```

This method skips past the next *n* bytes. It returns the actual number of bytes skipped.

```
public native int available() throws IOException;
```

This method returns the number of bytes which can be obtained from the stream without reading more data from the disk.

```
public native void close() throws IOException;
```

This method closes the file.

```
public void mark(int readlimit);
public void reset() throws IOException;
```

The *mark* method lets you mark the current location in the stream. If you later call *reset*, you will be returned to the marked location. *readLimit* is the maximum number of bytes you can read after calling *mark* before calling *reset*. If you read more bytes than this, you will no longer be able to call *reset*.

List (AWT)

This class lets you create List objects, which represent what Windows calls list box controls.

List is a sub-class of Component, so you can use any of the Component methods on a List object.

```
public List();
public List(int rows, boolean multipleSelections);
```

The second constructor creates a list that shows rows at a time. (If there are more than rows items in the list, scroll bars will let you see them all.) If multipleSelections is true, the user will be able to select any number of items from the list at once; if it is false, only one item can be selected at a time.

The first constructor creates a list which shows zero rows at a time and does not allow multiple selections. This kind of list is not very useful.

```
public int countItems();
```

This method returns the number of items in the list.

```
public String getItem(int index);
```

This method returns the text from the item with the given index. The index should be zero to return the first item in the list, one to return the second, and so on.

```
public synchronized void addItem(String item);
public synchronized void addItem(String item, int index);
```

These methods allow you to add items to the list. The first method adds to the end of the list, and the second at the specified index. (Thus, to make an item the second on the list, you would use an index of 1. This would cause all the items on the list, except the first one, to be moved down the list.)

```
public synchronized void replaceItem(String newValue, int index);
```

This will replace the text for the item at the given index. (The index should be zero to replace the first item, one to replace the second, and so on.)

```
public synchronized void clear();
```

This will remove all the items on the list.

```
public synchronized void delItem(int position);
public synchronized void delItems(int start, int end);
```

These methods allow you to remove items from the list. The first method will remove the item at the given position. (The position should be zero to remove the first item on the list, one to remove the second, and so on.) The second method will remove all the items between the given positions. For example, if you use *delItems(1,2)*, you would remove the second and third items on the list.

```
public synchronized String getSelectedItem();
public synchronized int getSelectedIndex();
```

These methods allow you to determine which item the user has selected. The first method returns the text of the selected item, and the second returns the index of the item. The index will be zero for the first item, one for the second, and so on. If no item is selected, the first method will return null and the second will return -1.

These methods are normally used only if the listbox is not set for multiple selections (i.e., if the user is only allowed to select one item at a time). However, it can be used even if multiple selections are allowed. In that case, the methods will work normally if only one item is selected, but they will return null and -1 if more than one item is selected.

```
public synchronized int[] getSelectedIndexes();
public synchronized String[] getSelectedItems();
```

These methods allow you to determine which items have been selected by the user. The first method returns an array of the indexes for the selected items. The indexes will be zero if the first item is selected, one if the second is selected, and so on. The second method returns an array of the text of the selected items. In both cases, you should use the *length* field variable for the array to determine how many items are on the list.

```
public synchronized void select(int index);
public synchronized void deselect(int index);
```

These methods allow you to select or deselect an item. The index should be zero to effect the first item, one to effect the second, and so on.

If multiple selections are allowed for the list (as determined in the constructor), calling these methods has no effect on whether or not other items in the list are selected. If multiple selections are not allowed, calling select will deselect the currently selected item.

Selecting an item doesn't automatically cause the list to be positioned so the item is visible. To do that, you should call *makeVisible*.

```
public synchronized boolean isSelected(int index);
```

This method tells you if the item at the given index is selected. The index should be zero to test the first item on the list, one to test the second, and so on.

```
public int getRows();
```

This method determines how many rows of the list will be visible at once. (The number of items on the list may be smaller or larger than this value.)

```
public boolean allowsMultipleSelections();
public void setMultipleSelections(boolean v);
```

These methods allow you to determine if multiple selections are allowed, and to change whether multiple selections are allowed. If multiple selections are not allowed, the user will only be able to select one item on the list at a time. If they are allowed, any number of items may be selected at a time.

```
public int getVisibleIndex();
```

This method returns the last index that was passed to the *makeVisible* method.

```
public void makeVisible(int index);
```

This method will scroll the list, if necessary, to insure that the item with the specified index is visible to the user. The index should be zero for the first item on the list, one for the second, and so on.

```
public Dimension preferredSize(int rows);
public Dimension preferredSize();
public Dimension minimumSize(int rows);
public Dimension minimumSize();
```

These methods allow you to determine the minimim and preferred size for the list. The methods without a parameter return the information for the current size of the control. The methods with a *rows* parameter return that information for the specified number of rows.

Long (lang)

Objects of this class are immutable. That means they are assigned a value when they are created, and that value cannot be changed later. If you want the object to have a different value, you must create a new object with that new value.

```
public static final long MIN_VALUE;
public static final long MAX_VALUE;
```

These are the minimum and maximum values a long may have.

```
public Long(long value);
public Long(String s) throws NumberFormatException;
```

These constructors allow you to create a Long object.

```
public static String toString(long i, int radix);
public static String toString(long i);
```

These convert the long to a String. The second form assumes a radix of 10.

```
public static long parseLong(String s, int radix) throws NumberFormatException;
public static long parseLong(String s) throws NumberFormatException;
public static Long valueOf(String s, int radix) throws NumberFormatException;
public static Long valueOf(String s) throws NumberFormatException;
```

These methods convert a String holding a long value. The first two create a long, and the second two create a Long. The forms without a *radix* parameter assume a radix of 10.

```
public int intValue();
public long longValue();
public float floatValue();
```

```
public double doubleValue();
public String toString();
```

These methods convert the Long to other types.

```
public boolean equals(Object obj);
```

This returns true if obj is a Long and it has the same numeric value.

Math (lang)

The Math class is simply a convenient way to combine together various math methods. You never create objects of this class.

```
public static final double E = 2.7182818284590452354;
public static final double PI = 3.14159265358979323846;
```

These are some useful numeric constants.

```
public static native double sin(double a);
public static native double cos(double a);
public static native double tan(double a);
public static native double asin(double a);
 public static native double acos(double a);
public static native double atan(double a);
public static native double exp(double a);
```

These methods provide various trigonometric functions.

```
public static native double log(double a) throws ArithmeticException;
```

This method returns the natural logarithm of a.

145

```
public static native double sqrt(double a) throws ArithmeticException;
```

This method returns the square root of a.

```
public static native double IEEEremainder(double f1, double f2);
```

This method returns the remainder left when $f1$ is divided by $f2$. Its name begins with IEEE because it follows the IEEE rules for division.

```
public static native double ceil(double a);
public static native double floor(double a);
```

The *ceil* method returns the nearest integer greater than or equal to a. The *floor* method returns the nearest integer less than or equal to a.

```
public static native double rint(double a);
```

This method converts a to an *int*, then returns that value as a double.

```
public static native double atan2(double a, double b);
```

This method converts the rectangular coordinates (a,b) to polar $(r,theta)$ and returns the result.

```
public static native double pow(double a, double b) throws ArithmeticException;
```

> This method returns *a* raised to the *b* power.

```
public static int round(float a);
public static long round(double a);
```

> These methods round *a* to the nearest integer.

```
public static synchronized double random();
```

> This method returns a random number in the range 0 to 1.

```
public static int abs(int a);
public static long abs(long a);
public static float abs(float a);
public static double abs(double a);
```

> These methods return the absolute value of *a*.

```
public static int max(int a, int b);
public static long max(long a, long b);
public static float max(float a, float b);
public static double max(double a, double b);
```

> These methods return *a* or *b*, whichever is larger.

```
public static int min(int a, int b);
public static long min(long a, long b);
public static float min(float a, float b);
public static double min(double a, double b);
```

> These methods return *a* or *b*, whichever is smaller.

146

MediaTracker (AWT)

> The MediaTracker class allows you to track the progress of Image objects as they are downloaded from the Internet. This tracking isn't necessary, since the images will automatically be painted on the screen when they arrive. It can provide information to your program about the progress of that downloading, however, and it can be used to cause other things to happen as soon as an image is ready.

```
public static final int LOADING;
public static final int ABORTED;
public static final int COMPLETE;
```

> These values provide the status of an image. These values are returned by several of the methods of this class, often or'ed together if more than one status applies.

```
public MediaTracker(Component comp);
```

> This constructor lets you create MediaTracker objects. Each object can track several images, but applies only to one Component object (such as an Applet).

```
public void addImage(Image image, int id);
public synchronized void addImage(Image image, int id, int w, int h);
```

These methods add a new image to the list of images the MediaTracker object is tracking. Each image is given an *id* value, which can be used later to identify that image. That value can be unique, but doesn't have to be.

```
public boolean checkAll();
public synchronized boolean checkAll(boolean load);
```

These methods return true if all of the images have finished their loading process. (That doesn't necessarily mean they loaded successfully—even if the process ended in an error, it is still considered to have ended.)

The second version of the method can have a value of true for load if you want to cause any images that haven't started the loading process to begin.

```
public synchronized boolean isErrorAny();
```

This will return true if any of the images have stopped loading due to an error.

```
public synchronized Object[] getErrorsAny();
```

This returns an array of all the image objects (if any) that have stopped loading due to an error.

```
public void waitForAll() throws InterruptedException;
public synchronized boolean waitForAll(long ms);
```

These methods will wait until all the images have finished their loading (either successfully or unsuccessfully). The second version of the method will wait no more than *ms* milliseconds.

147

```
public int statusID(int id, boolean load);
public int statusAll(boolean load);
```

This method returns an integer containing an or'ed combination of the status of one or more images. The first version returns the status of all the images with the given *id*. The second version returns the status of all the images. Each status is one of the constants listed at the beginning of this class.

If load is true, the loading process will begin for the specified images if it hasn't already.

```
public boolean checkID(int id);
public synchronized boolean checkID(int id, boolean load);
```

These methods determine whether or not all the images with the specified *id* value have completed their loading process (either successfully or unsuccessfully). If load is true, the loading will be started for any images which have not yet started.

```
public synchronized boolean isErrorID(int id);
public synchronized Object[] getErrorsID(int id);
```

These methods allow you to check for images which failed to load due to an error. The first method will return true if any of the methods with the specified *id* have failed. The second returns a list of the images with that *id* which have failed.

```
public void waitForID(int id) throws InterruptedException;
```

> This method will wait until all the images with the given *id* have finished loading (either successfully or unsuccessfully). Calling it will start loading any images with that *id* which have not yet started to load.

MemoryImageSource (AWT.Image)

> This class is a type of ImageProducer. It produces the image by taking a set of pixels passed to it and making an Image from it. This class would not be used directly in a program which is simply displaying an image; like most of the classes in AWT.Image, it is used only for the unusual case in which image manipulation is to be done.

```
public MemoryImageSource(int w, int h, ColorModel cm, byte[] pix, int off, int scan);
public MemoryImageSource(int w, int h, ColorModel cm, byte[] pix, int off, int scan, ⇐
Hashtable props);
public MemoryImageSource(int w, int h, ColorModel cm, int[] pix, int off, int scan);
public MemoryImageSource(int w, int h, ColorModel cm, int[] pix, int off, int scan, ⇐
Hashtable props);
public MemoryImageSource(int w, int h, int pix[], int off, int scan);
public MemoryImageSource(int w, int h, int pix[], int off, int scan, Hashtable props);
public synchronized void addConsumer(ImageConsumer ic);
public synchronized boolean isConsumer(ImageConsumer ic);
public synchronized void removeConsumer(ImageConsumer ic);
public void startProduction(ImageConsumer ic);
public void requestTopDownLeftRightResend(ImageConsumer ic);
```

Menu (AWT)

> This class is a sub-class of MenuItem and MenuComponent, so you can use the methods from them as well as the ones listed below for Menu objects.
>
> Remember the hierarchy for menu classes: the highest level is a MenuBar. There will be just one of those objects in a frame at a time. That object references a series of Menu objects (e.g., a Menu object for the File menu, one for the Edit menu, etc.). Each Menu object references a series of MenuItem objects (e.g., a MenuItem object for Open, one for New, one for Save, etc.).

```
public Menu(String label);
public Menu(String label, boolean tearOff);
```

> These constructors allow you to create Menu items. The label is the text that appears on the menu bar to identify the menu. The *tearOff* parameter indicates whether or not the menu can be torn off (i.e., whether you can press the mouse down in the menu and then drag it to a location where it will permanently be displayed). This feature isn't available on all platforms, and is not available on Windows.

```
public boolean isTearOff();
```

> This method tells you if the menu was created with the *tearOff* parameter to the constructor set to true.

```
public int countItems();
```

This method returns the number of MenuItem objects associated with the menu.

```
public MenuItem getItem(int index);
```

This method lets you obtain the item in position index on the menu. The index would be zero to obtain the first item, one to obtain the second, and so on.

```
public synchronized MenuItem add(MenuItem mi);
public void add(String label);
public void addSeparator();
```

These methods let you add new items to the menu. It is normally simpler to use the second method than the first. The third method adds a separator line across the menu. All of these methods add the new item to the end of the menu.

```
public synchronized void remove(int index);
public synchronized void remove(MenuComponent item);
```

These methods remove an item from the menu.

The first method removes the item at the specified index. It should be zero to remove the first item, one to remove the second, and so on.

The second method removes the specified item. The item should be the same item (not just an item with the same text) as the one to be removed.

MenuBar (AWT)

This class is a sub-class of MenuComponent, so you can use the methods from that class as well as the ones listed below to operate on MenuBar objects.

149

Remember the hierarchy for menu classes: The highest level is a MenuBar. There will be just one of those objects in a frame at a time. That object references a series of Menu objects (e.g., a Menu object for the File menu, one for the Edit menu, etc.). Each Menu object references a series of MenuItem objects (e.g., a MenuItem object for Open, one for New, one for Save, etc.).

```
public MenuBar();
```

This constructor lets you create MenuBar objects.

```
public Menu getHelpMenu();
public synchronized void setHelpMenu(Menu m);
```

These methods let you get and set the help menu. On some platforms, such as Windows, this has no effect.

```
public synchronized Menu add(Menu m);
public synchronized void remove(int index);
public synchronized void remove(MenuComponent m);
```

These methods let you add and remove menus from the menu bar.

If you use the first version of remove, the index should be zero to remove the first menu, one to remove the second, and so on.

If you use the second version of remove, the *m* should be a Menu which was previously added to the menu bar. (It shouldn't just be a Menu with the same items, but should be the very same object.)

```
public int countMenus();
```

This method returns the number of menus on the menu bar.

```
public Menu getMenu(int index);
```

This method returns the menu with the specified index. The index should be zero to obtain the first menu, one to obtain the second one, and so on.

MenuComponent (AWT)

This is an abstract class which is the super-class to MenuBar and MenuItem. Since it is an abstract class, you never create objects of type MenuComponent.

```
public MenuContainer getParent();
```

This method returns a Menu if used on a MenuItem object, and it returns a MenuBar if used on a Menu item.

```
public Font getFont();
public void setFont(Font f);
```

These methods let you set or get the font to be used for the MenuBar, Menu, or MenuItem.

150

```
public boolean postEvent(Event evt);
```

This lets you send an event to the MenuBar, Menu, or MenuItem.

```
public String toString();
```

This will convert the GridLayout object to a String. This can be helpful in debugging a program, especially if the String is then passed to System.out.println.

MenuContainer (AWT)

This is an interface used by the Menu, MenuBar, and Frame classes. It represents things which can contain objects of type MenuComponent.

Since it is an interface, it has no methods that are not also provided by its subordinate classes, so they are described in the subordinate classes.

MenuItem (AWT)

This class is a sub-class of MenuComponent, so you can use the methods from that class as well as those listed below when operating on a MenuItem object.

Remember the hierarchy for menu classes: the highest level is a MenuBar. There will be just one of those objects in a frame at a time. That object references a series of Menu objects (e.g., a Menu object for the File menu, one for the Edit menu, etc.). Each Menu object references a series of MenuItem objects (e.g., a MenuItem object for Open, one for New, one for Save, etc.).

Items of the CheckboxMenuItem class can be used in place of MenuItem objects if the item is to be checkable.

```
public MenuItem(String label);
```

This constructor allows you to create MenuItem objects.

```
public String getLabel();
public void setLabel(String label);
```

These methods let you get and set the text that appears on the menu for this menu item.

```
public boolean isEnabled();
public void enable();
public void enable(boolean cond);
public void disable();
```

These methods let you determine if a menu item is enabled or disabled, and to enable or disable the item.

Object (lang)

This is an unusual class. All classes declared in Java are sub-classes of this class, either directly or indirectly. If you declare a class in Java and don't include an extends clause in the class header, the Java compiler will automatically put extends Object there. As a result, the methods provided by this class can be performed on any Java object.

151

```
public final native Class getClass();
```

This method returns the Class object that describes the class to which the object belongs.

```
public boolean equals(Object obj);
```

This method is available for all objects, but it doesn't work very well unless the lowest sub-class overrides it. That is because the version in the Object class can't really compare the contents of the two objects, so it simply checks to see if the two variables reference the same object. If they do, it returns true; if not, it returns false.

```
public String toString();
```

This creates a String that describes the object. It doesn't work well unless the lowest sub-class overrides it. That is because the version in the Object class doesn't really know very much about the object, so it can't put much useful information in the String.

```
public final native void wait(long timeout) throws InterruptedException;
public final void wait(long timeout, int nanos) throws InterruptedException;
public final void wait() throws InterruptedException;
```

These methods cause the execution of the current thread to be suspended. The first two versions cause it to be suspended for the specified time, and the last causes it to be suspended indefinitely. These methods can only be used in methods which are synchronized.

The *timeout* parameter is the amount of time to wait in milliseconds. If there is a *nanos* parameter, it provides the additional number of nanoseconds to wait.

In addition to resuming if the time expires, the threads will also resume execution if notify or notifyAll is called.

```
public final native void notify();
public final native void notifyAll();
```

These methods cause a thread that has been suspended by calling *wait* to resume execution. The first version will only resume a single thread, while the second version will resume all threads that are waiting.

```
public int hashCode();
```

This method is used if the objects of the class will be placed in a table implemented with the Hashtable class. It should return an integer which identifies the object. The integer doesn't have to be absolutely unique—two or more different objects could share the same integer value. But the integer should be reasonably unique (i.e., there shouldn't be too many objects which share any given integer).

Observable (util)

152

Suppose you have a class of objects (call them observables), and whenever a change occurs to one of those objects there are several other objects (call them observers) which want to be notified. (What they do about that change is up to them—your concern is simply to notify them that the change has taken place.) You can use the Observable and Observer classes to accomplish this.

First, you will want the Observable class to be a super-class of the class of objects which may change (the observable objects). Whenever one of those objects changes, all the observer objects must be notified. Those observer objects would all be in classes which implements Observer.

```
public synchronized void addObserver(Observer observer);
public synchronized void deleteObserver(Observer observer);
public synchronized void deleteObservers();
```

These methods let you add or remove an observer from the list of observers for the current object.

```
public void notifyObservers();
public synchronized void notifyObservers(Object arg);
```

These methods check to see if a change to the object has taken place (i.e., if setChanged has been called). If it has, this method notifies all the observers of the change. (It does this by calling the *update* method for each of the Observer objects.) It then clears the changed flag (by calling clearChanged).

When the *update* method is called, it can be passed an *arg* which provides information about the change. If the first version of notifyObservers is used, null is passed to *update* for the *arg* parameter.

```
public synchronized boolean hasChanged();
```

This returns true if the object has been changed, and the observers have not yet been notified (i.e., if setChanged has been called, but notifyObservers hasn't been called).

```
public synchronized int countObservers();
```

This method returns the number of Observer objects for this Observable object.

```
protected synchronized void setChanged();
protected synchronized void clearChanged();
```

These methods allow you to set and clear the flag that indicates that the object has been changed. Notice that they are *protected* methods, so they can only be called by methods of this class and its sub-classes (which would include the class which is Observable).

Observer (util)

This interface must be implemented by any object which wants to observe changes in other objects. See the Observable class for details.

```
void update(Observable obj, Object arg);
```

If a change takes place in the object being observed, this method will be called. The *obj* parameter specifies the object which changed, and the *arg* is the parameter sent to the *notifyObservers* method.

OutputStream (io)

This is an abstract class which groups together all the various forms of output streams: ByteArrayOutputStream, FileOutputStream, FilterOutputStream, and PipedInputStream. Those sub-classes override most of the methods of this class, so they are listed in the sub-classes rather than here.

Panel (AWT)

Panel objects are often used in dialogs and frames as areas in which various controls are placed. Because each Panel can have its own layout manager, this gives you additional flexibility over how the layout for an entire dialog or frame is done.

Panel is a sub-class of Container, and Component, so you can use methods from either of those classes, as well as those listed below, to control a Panel object.

```
public Panel();
```

This constructor lets you create Panel objects.

PipedInputStream (io)

This class works in conjunction with the PipedOutputStream class. Together, they allow data to be sent over a stream between two threads. One thread will have a PipedOutputStream object to which it is sending data. That data will be received by the other thread on a PipedInputStream object.

```
public PipedInputStream ();
public PipedInputStream (PipedOutputStream src) throws IOException;
```

These constructors let you create a PipedInputStream object. The first version doesn't connect it to a PipedOutputStream object. As a result, you will need to use the *connect* method before you can read data from the stream.

```
public void connect(PipedOutputStream src) throws IOException;
```

This connects the PipedInputStream to a PipedOutputStream.

```
public synchronized int read() throws IOException;
public synchronized int read(byte b[]) throws IOException;
public synchronized int read(byte b[], int off, int len) throws IOException;
```

These methods let you read data from the stream. (The stream must be connected to a PipedInputStream object, either by specifying one in the constructor or by calling *connect*, before this can be done.) The first version reads and returns a single byte from the stream. The second version reads up to *b.length* bytes into array *b*. The third version reads up to *len* bytes into array *b* starting at index off.

154

There may be a significant delay between the time you call this method and the time it returns. That is because the method may have to wait for more data to be sent down the stream before it can return the data to you.

```
public long skip(long n) throws IOException;
```

This method skips *n* bytes in the stream. It returns the actual number of bytes skipped.

```
public void close()  throws IOException;
```

This method closes the stream.

PipedOutputStream (io)

This class works in conjunction with the PipedInputStream class. Together, they allow data to be sent over a stream between two threads. One thread will have a PipedOutputStream object to which it is sending data. That data will be received by the other thread on a PipedInputStream object.

```
public PipedOutputStream(PipedInputStream snk)  throws IOException;
public PipedOutputStream();
```

These constructors let you create a PipedOutputStream object. The first version connects that object with the specified PipedInputStream object. The second version creates a stream which is not connected; it must be connected by calling connect before it can be used.

```
public void connect(PipedInputStream snk) throws IOException;
```

This method connects the PipedOutputStream object to the specified PipedInputStream object.

```
public void write(int b) throws IOException;
public void write(byte b[]) throws IOException;
public void write(byte b[], int off, int len) throws IOException;
```

These methods let you write data to the stream. The first will write a single byte of data. The second will write *b.length* bytes from array *b*. The third will write *len* bytes from array *b* starting at index off.

```
public void close() throws IOException;
```

This method will close the stream.

```
public void flush() throws IOException;
```

This method has no effect.

PixelGrabber (AWT.Image)

The PixelGrabber class is a type of ImageConsumer. It can be attached to an ImageProducer, and convert the image it produces into a series of pixels. This class would not be used directly in a program which is simply displaying an image; like most of the classes in AWT.Image, it is used only for the unusual case in which image manipulation is to be done.

155

```
public PixelGrabber(Image img, int x, int y, int w, int h, int[] pix, int off, ⇐
int scansize);
public PixelGrabber(ImageProducer ip, int x, int y, int w, int h, int[] pix, int off, ⇐
int scansize);
public boolean grabPixels() throws InterruptedException;
public synchronized boolean grabPixels(long ms) throws InterruptedException;
public synchronized int status();
public void setDimensions(int width, int height);
public void setHints(int hints);
public void setProperties(Hashtable props);
public void setColorModel(ColorModel model);
public void setPixels(int srcX, int srcY, int srcW, int srcH, ColorModel model, ⇐
byte pixels[], int srcOff, int srcScan);
public void setPixels(int srcX, int srcY, int srcW, int srcH, ColorModel model, ⇐
int pixels[], int srcOff, int srcScan);
public synchronized void imageComplete(int status);
```

Point (AWT)

This class identifies a particular point within a Component. It does this by specifying the x-coordinate (i.e., how far to go from the left-hand edge) and the y-coordinate (i.e., how far to go from the top). Objects of this class are used by a variety of Java methods.

```
public int x;
public int y;
```

These field variables specify the x-coordinate and y-coordinate of the point.

```
public Point(int x, int y);
```

This constructor allows you to create a *Point* object.

```
public void move(int x, int y);
public void translate(int x, int y);
```

The *move* method changes the point to the specified *x* and *y* value. The *translate* method changes the x-coordinate by *x*, and changes the y-coordinate by *y*.

```
public boolean equals(Object object);
```

This method returns true if the object is a Point, and if it has the same x- and y-coordinates.

```
public String toString();
```

156

This will convert the Point object to a String. This can be helpful in debugging a program, especially if the String is then passed to System.out.println.

Polygon (AWT)

Objects of this class are used by the *drawPolygon* and *fillPolygon* methods of the Graphics class.

```
public int npoints;
public int xpoints[];
public int ypoints[];
```

These field variables identify the number of points in the polygon, and the x- and y-coordinates for the points.

```
public Polygon();
public Polygon(int xpoints[], int ypoints[], int npoints);
```

These constructors let you create an empty polygon or a polygon with the specified points.

```
public void addPoint(int x, int y);
```

This method adds a new point to the polygon.

```
public Rectangle getBoundingBox();
```

This method finds the smallest rectangle that will completely enclose the polygon.

```
public boolean inside(int x, int y);
```

This method returns true if the specified point is inside the polygon.

PrintStream (io)

This method is a type of OutputStream which has methods that allow easy generation of lines of text. (It is generally easier to generate lines of text with PrintStream than with DataOutputStream.)

One common object of this class is System.out. It can be a convenient place to output debugging information.

```
public PrintStream(OutputStream out);
public PrintStream(OutputStream out, boolean autoflush);
```

These constructors let you create an object of this class. The *autoflush* parameter indicates whether or not the stream will be flushed after each complete line is printed. (The default for this value is false.)

```
public void write(int b);
public void write(byte b[]);
public void write(byte b[], int off, int len);
```

These methods let you write bytes of data to the stream. Although it is legal to use these methods, it would be more common to use *print* and *println*.

```
public void flush();
```

This sends any data being held in temporary output buffers to the stream.

157

```
public void close();
```

This method closes the stream.

```
public boolean checkError();
```

This method returns true if an error has occurred on the stream. (Once an error occurs, the condition persists, so this method will continue to return true.)

```
public void print(Object obj);
synchronized public void print(String s);
synchronized public void print(char s[]);
public void print(char c);
public void print(int i);
public void print(long l);
public void print(float f);
public void print(double d);
public void print(boolean b);
```

These methods write data to the stream. Regardless of the type of data sent to the method, the data will be converted to text before being sent to the stream.

```
public void println();
```

This method sends an end-of-line sequence to the stream.

```
synchronized public void println(Object obj);
synchronized public void println(String s);
synchronized public void println(char s[]);
synchronized public void println(char c);
synchronized public void println(int i);
synchronized public void println(long l);
synchronized public void println(float f);
synchronized public void println(double d);
synchronized public void println(boolean b);
```

These methods perform the same function as the corresponding *print* method, but they also send an end-of-line sequence to the stream.

Process (lang)

Objects of this class are returned by the *exec* methods in the System class. They represent newly-created processes. This class provides methods that let you control those processes.

```
public OutputStream getOutputStream();
public InputStream getInputStream();
public InputStream getErrorStream();
```

These methods allow your process to use a stream that is connected to a stream in the new process. getOutputStream will create an OutputStream in your process that is connected to the System.in stream in the new process. getInputStream will create an InputStream in your process that is connected to the System.out stream in the new process. getErrorStream will create an InputStream in your process that is connected to the System.err stream in the new process.

```
public int waitFor() throws InterruptedException;
```

This method causes execution of your process to be suspended until the new process terminates. When it terminates, the *waitFor* method will return the code passed to the *System.exit* method in the new process.

```
public int exitValue();
```

This method returns the code passed to the *System.exit* method in the new process. It will generate an IllegalThreadStateException if the other process has not yet terminated.

```
public void destroy();
```

This will terminate the new process.

Properties (util)

This class is basically a Hashtable which contains a list of properties. Each property has a name (its key) and a value. The important thing this class does is to allow you to store those properties in a disk file.

Because this class is a sub-class of the Hashtable class, you can use all the methods in Hashtable on its objects.

```
public Properties();
public Properties(Properties defaults);
```

These constructors let you create objects of the Properties class.

The second method says that the defaults object contains default values for some (or all) of the property keys. When you call getProperty, the default should be used if the property list doesn't have a value for that key.

```
public synchronized void load(InputStream in) throws IOException;
public synchronized void save(OutputStream out, String header);
```

These methods let you load the properties from a stream, or save them to a stream.

```
public String getProperty(String key);
public String getProperty(String key, String defaultValue);
```

These methods let you look for a given property. If it finds one with the key value, it will return that property. If it doesn't, it will try to use a default.

The first version of the method will use the default provided by the constructor (if there was one).

The second version of the method will use the defaultValue supplied.

```
public Enumeration propertyNames();
```

This method creates an Enumeration object which lets you get each of the property names (i.e., the keys).

159

PushbackInputStream (io)

This is a perfectly ordinary InputStream, except for the fact that it includes the *unread* method.

```
public PushbackInputStream(InputStream in);
```

This constructor lets you create an object of the PushbackInputStream class.

```
public int read() throws IOException;
public int read(byte bytes[]) throws IOException;
public int read(byte bytes[], int offset, int length) throws IOException;
```

These methods let you read data from the stream. The first method reads a single byte. The second method reads up to *b.length* bytes into array *b*. The third reads up to *length* bytes into array *b* starting at index offset. The second and third methods return the number of bytes actually read. They will all return -1 if the end of the stream is reached before any data is read.

These methods will all read just one byte if *unread* has been called since the last call to *read*.

```
public void unread(int ch) throws IOException;
```

  This method will cause *ch* to be the next byte read from the stream. You can only call this method once before calling *read* to read the byte.

```
public int available() throws IOException;
```

  This method tells you how many bytes of data can be read from the stream without waiting for a disk or network read operation.

```
public void close() throws IOException;
```

  This method will close the stream.

```
public long skip(long n) throws IOException;
```

  This method will skip past the next *n* bytes in the stream. It will return the number of bytes skipped.

Random (util)

  This method lets you create random numbers. Unless you are very serious about your random numbers, you may want to use the *random* method in the Math class—it is simpler to use.

```
public Random();
public Random(long seed);
```

  These constructors let you create an object of the Random class. The first method will use the time-of-day to generate a seed, while the second lets you specify the seed.

```
synchronized public void setSeed(long seed);
```

  This method lets you specify the seed.

```
public int nextInt();
public long nextLong();
public float nextFloat();
public double nextDouble();
synchronized public double nextGaussian();
```

  These methods let you obtain the next number in the random series. *nextInt* and *nextLong* will generate numbers uniformly distributed among the possible values for *int* and *long*. *nextFload* and *nextDouble* will generate numbers uniformly distributed over the range from 0.0 to 1.0. *nextGaussian* will return a Gaussian distributed number with mean 0.0 and standard deviation 1.0.

RandomAccessFile (io)

  All the other classes in the *io* package deal with streams. This class is the only exception.

  With streams, you must (for the most part) read the data in the sequence it is presented, or write the data in the sequence it is to be sent. You can't jump around from one point to another in the stream. The RandomAccessFile class allows you to jump around in a disk file with the *seek* method.

Another significant difference with a RandomAccessFile object is that you can use the same object to both read and write a file. With streams, you are either reading or writing, but cannot do both.

```
public RandomAccessFile(String name, String mode) throws IOException;
public RandomAccessFile(File file, String mode) throws IOException;
```

These methods let you create a RandomAccessFile object. The *name* identifies the file, and can be a simple name, a relative pathname, or a complete pathname. If you prefer, you can specify the filename with a File object. The *mode* should be either *r* or *rw*. The former means that you will only be reading the file, while the latter allows both reading and writing.

```
public final FileDescriptor getFD() throws IOException;
```

This allows you to obtain a FileDescriptor object for the file. There is rarely a need to do this.

```
public native int read() throws IOException;;
public int read(byte b[], int off, int len) throws IOException;
public int read(byte b[]) throws IOException;
```

These methods let you read bytes from the file. The first will read and return one byte. The second will read up to *len* bytes into array *b* starting with index off. The third will read up to *b.length* bytes into array *b*. The second and third methods will return the number of bytes actually read. All three methods will return -1 if no data could be read before the end of the file was reached.

These methods will not necessarily read the amount of data requested. They may read fewer bytes, because those bytes are easily available and more data is not. If you want to read all the data requested, use *readFully*.

```
public final void readFully(byte b[]) throws IOException;
public final void readFully(byte b[], int off, int len) throws IOException;
```

These methods work like the corresponding *read* methods except that they will wait (if necessary) for additional data to become available so that they can pass the full amount of data requested back to the caller. The only reason that fewer bytes would be returned is if the end of the file is reached.

```
public int skipBytes(int n) throws IOException;
```

This method will skip past the next *n* bytes in the file. The actual number of bytes skipped will be returned.

```
public native void write(int b) throws IOException;
public void write(byte b[]) throws IOException;
public void write(byte b[], int off, int len) throws IOException;
```

These methods will write data to the file. The first will write one byte. The second will write the *b.length* bytes from array *b*. The third will write *length* bytes from array *b* starting at index off.

```
public native long getFilePointer() throws IOException;
```

This method will return the current position in the file, measured in bytes from the beginning of the file. Thus, if you are at the beginning of the file (which means the next *write* would write the first byte in the file, or the next *read* would read the first byte in the file), this method will return zero.

```
public native void seek(long pos) throws IOException;
```

This method will move to the given position in the file. The position is measured in bytes from the beginning of the file. Thus, if you use *seek(2)*, the next *read* will read the third byte in the file, or the next *write* would write the third byte in the file.

```
public native long length() throws IOException;
```

This method returns the number of bytes currently in the file.

```
public native void close() throws IOException;
```

This method closes the file.

```
public final boolean readBoolean() throws IOException;
public final byte readByte() throws IOException;
public final int readUnsignedByte() throws IOException;
public final short readShort() throws IOException;
public final int readUnsignedShort() throws IOException;
public final char readChar() throws IOException;
public final int readInt() throws IOException;
public final long readLong() throws IOException;
public final float readFloat() throws IOException;
public final double readDouble() throws IOException;
public final String readLine() throws IOException;
public final String readUTF() throws IOException;
```

These methods read various kinds of data from the file. To insure that the data is in the proper form, it is best to read it using the method that corresponds to the one the data was written with. For example, if a certain part of the stream was written with the *writeLong* method, then you would read it with *readLong*. (Other methods might work, but are not guaranteed.)

The *readUTF* method reads character data which has been written in the special UTF format. This format places data in a form in which Latin characters take just one byte, rather than the two bytes that a Unicode character takes. The tradeoff for this savings is that non-Latin characters (such as Chinese characters) may take more than the two bytes a Unicode character normally takes. There is a *writeUTF* method that can be used to write data in this format.

```
public final void writeBoolean(boolean v) throws IOException;
public final void writeByte(int v) throws IOException;
public final void writeShort(int v) throws IOException;
public final void writeChar(int v) throws IOException;
public final void writeInt(int v) throws IOException;
public final void writeLong(long v) throws IOException;
public final void writeFloat(float v) throws IOException;
```

```
public final void writeDouble(double v) throws IOException;
public final void writeBytes(String s) throws IOException;
public final void writeChars(String s) throws IOException;
public final void writeUTF(String str) throws IOException;
```

These methods let you write data to the file. You can later read the data by using the corresponding read method. For example, if a certain part of the stream was written with the *writeLong* method, you would read it with *readLong*. (Other methods might work, but are not guaranteed.)

The *writeUTF* method writes character data in the special UTF format. This format places data in a form in which Latin characters take just one byte, rather than the two bytes that a Unicode character takes. The tradeoff for this savings is that non-Latin characters (such as Chinese characters) may take more than the two bytes a Unicode character normally takes. The *readUTF* method will read data in this format.

Rectangle (AWT)

Objects of the Rectangle class are used by a variety of Java methods.

```
public int x;
public int y;
public int width;
public int height;
```

These field variables describe the location and size of the rectangle.

```
public Rectangle();
public Rectangle(int x, int y, int width, int height);
public Rectangle(int width, int height);
public Rectangle(Point p, Dimension d);
public Rectangle(Point p);
public Rectangle(Dimension d);
```

These constructors allow you to create a new rectangle in a variety of ways. The first method creates an empty rectangle. The third and last methods create a rectangle at position (0,0). The fifth method creates a rectangle with zero height and width.

```
public void reshape(int x, int y, int width, int height);
```

This method lets you change the position and size of the rectangle.

```
public void move(int x, int y);
public void translate(int x, int y);
```

These methods let you change the position of the rectangle. The first method moves the rectangle to the specified position, and the second method moves it by x horizontally and moves it by y vertically.

```
public void resize(int width, int height);
```

This method lets you change the size of the rectangle.

```
public boolean inside(int x, int y);
```

This method returns true if the point is inside the rectangle.

```
public boolean intersects(Rectangle r);
public Rectangle intersection(Rectangle r);
public Rectangle union(Rectangle r);
```

These methods deal with how two rectangles intersect. The first returns true if the rectangles intersect. The second returns a rectangle that describes the area of intersection between the two rectangles. The third returns a rectangle that completely encloses the first two rectangles.

```
public void add(int newx, int newy);
public void add(Point pt);
public void add(Rectangle r);
```

These methods increase the size of the rectangle. The first two methods increase the size so it includes the given point. The last method increases the size so it includes the specified rectangle.

```
public void grow(int h, int v);
```

This method moves the top and bottom of the rectangle to increase it in both directions by *v*. It moves the left and right edges of the rectangle to increase it in both directions by *h*. If *h* or *v* is negative, the rectangle will decrease in size in that dimension, rather than increasing.

164

```
public boolean isEmpty();
```

This method returns true if the width and height of the rectangle are both zero (or negative).

```
public boolean equals(Object obj);
```

This method returns true if the obj is a Rectangle and if it has the same size and position.

```
public String toString();
```

This will convert the Rectangle object to a String. This can be helpful in debugging a program, especially if the String is then passed to System.out.println.

RGBImageFilter (AWT.Image)

This is a sub-class of the ImageFilter class, and provides a mechanism that allows you to filter an image by processing each pixel one at a time. This would be appropriate, for example, if you wanted to change all blue pixels to red. Sub-classes do this by providing a *filterRGB* method. This class would not be used directly in a program which is simply displaying an image; like most of the classes in AWT.Image, it is used only for the unusual case in which image manipulation is to be done.

```
public void substituteColorModel(ColorModel oldcm, ColorModel newcm);
public IndexColorModel filterIndexColorModel(IndexColorModel icm);
public void filterRGBPixels(int x, int y, int w, int h, int pixels[], int off, ⇐
int scansize);
```

```
public void setPixels(int x, int y, int w, int h, ColorModel model, byte pixels[], ⇐
int off, int scansize);
public void setPixels(int x, int y, int w, int h, ColorModel model, int pixels[], ⇐
int off, int scansize);
public int filterRGB(int x, int y, int rgb);
```

Runnable (lang)

This is an interface which allows an object (most commonly an Applet object) to include a *run* method which will execute as a separate thread. This provides a simple way to run as a thread without the more involved process of creating a sub-class of the Thread class.

```
public abstract void run();
```

This is the only method in the interface. Any class which implements Runnable must provide this method.

Runtime (lang)

There is always exactly one object of this class, where you can obtain a reference to the *getRuntime* method. The methods in the class allow you to perform system operations, such as creating new processes.

```
public static Runtime getRuntime();
```

This method returns a reference to the single Runtime object. You cannot create Runtime objects, but you can do what you need to by using the object returned by this method.

165

```
public void exit(int status);
```

This causes the Java virtual machine to terminate.

```
public Process exec(String command) throws IOException;
public Process exec(String command, String envp[]) throws IOException;
public Process exec(String cmdarray[]) throws IOException;
public Process exec(String cmdarray[], String envp[]) throws IOException;
```

These methods create a new process. The *command* and *cmdarray* parameters specify the system command to be executed to start the new process. The envp array is an array of strings, each of which specifies one environment parameter. For example, a string might be debug=true to give the environment variable *debug* a value of true.

These methods return a Process object, which can be used to control the new process and connect streams to it.

```
public native long freeMemory();
public native long totalMemory();
```

These methods return the number of bytes in the Java system memory, and the amount of that memory which is currently free.

```
public native void gc();
```

> This method calls the Java garbage collector. It locates objects which are no longer in use, and returns the memory they occupy to the free memory pool. The garbage collector runs automatically at regular intervals, so there is rarely a need to run it directly by calling this method.

```
public native void runFinalization();
```

> This method causes the *finalize* method for any objects which are being destroyed to be run. It is rarely necessary to cause this to happen, since it will happen automatically on its own.

```
public native void traceInstructions(boolean on);
public native void traceMethodCalls(boolean on);
```

> In some environments, these methods turn on (or off) a debugging trace of each statement, or each method call.

```
public synchronized void load(String filename);
public synchronized void loadLibrary(String libname);
```

> These methods let you load a library that contains *native* methods. (Methods implemented in another language, such as C++, must be placed in libraries. On Windows, those libraries take the form of .dll's.)

```
public InputStream getLocalizedInputStream(InputStream in);
public OutputStream getLocalizedOutputStream(OutputStream out);
```

> These methods let you create streams which translate between Unicode (used by Java) and the character type used by the native system (which may not be Unicode).

RuntimeExceptions

Listed below are all the standard Java runtime exceptions. The non-runtime exceptions are not listed here—they are listed under the Exceptions heading.

You can create your own exceptions by creating a class which is a sub-class of Exception or RuntimeException classes.

Remember that you must handle the exception if you call a method which throws an exception which is not a RuntimeException. On the other hand, if a method throws a RuntimeException, you may handle it or not—as you wish.

```
ArithmeticException
ArrayIndexOutOfBoundsException
ArrayStoreException
ClassCastException
EmptyStackException
IllegalArgumentException
IllegalMonitorStateException
IllegalThreadStateException
IndexOutOfBoundsException
NegativeArraySizeException
NoSuchElementException
NullPointerException
NumberFormatException
```

```
SecurityException
StringIndexOutOfBoundsException
```

Scrollbar (AWT)

This class lets you create objects that represent scrollbar controls.

Scrollbar is a sub-class of Component, so you can use any of the Component methods on a Scrollbar object.

```
public static final int HORIZONTAL;
public static final int VERTICAL;
```

These are used by the constructor to indicate the kind of scrollbar.

```
public Scrollbar();
public Scrollbar(int orientation);
public Scrollbar(int orientation, int value, int visible, int minimum, int maximum);
```

The first and second constructors are not very useful unless you intend to set the other information later with setValues. The first constructor will create a vertical scrollbar.

The *value* parameter specifies the current value the scrollbar should have. It should always be at least *minimum*, and should not exceed *maximum-visible*.

The *visible* parameter specifies the number of positions that are visible to the user at once. This parameter affects the height of the scrollbar thumb on some platforms. On all platforms, it affects the largest value the scrollbar can reach, which is *maximum-visible*.

The *minimum* and *maximum* parameters set the range of the scrollbar. Keep in mind, though, that the user won't actually be able to move the scrollbar to get a value of *maximum*. The largest value that can actually be achieved is *maximum-visible*.

```
public int getOrientation();
```

This method returns either Scrollbar.HORIZONTAL or Scrollbar.VERTICAL, to tell you the orientation of the bar.

```
public int getValue();
```

This method returns the current value of the scrollbar. This value will change as the user operates the scrollbar.

```
public void setValue(int value);
```

This method will set the current value of the scrollbar. The scrollbar will be redrawn to show the thumb in the appropriate position.

```
public int getMinimum();
public int getMaximum();
public int getVisible();
```

These methods return the *minimum*, *maximum* and *visible* parameters for the scrollbar. These options can be set by the constructor or by setValues. For a description of their meanings, see the description of the constructor.

```
public void setLineIncrement(int l);
public int getLineIncrement();
```

These methods let you get and set the line increment. The line increment is the number of positions the scrollbar moves each time the user clicks on the arrows at either end of the bar. By default, the line increment is 1.

```
public void setPageIncrement(int l);
public int getPageIncrement();
```

These methods let you get and set the page increment. The page increment is the number of positions the scroll bar moves each time the user clicks in the gray area of the scroll bar next to the thumb. (This commonly moves the display by one page.) By default, the page increment is 10.

```
public void setValues(int value, int visible, int minimum, int maximum);
```

This method changes the parameters for the scrollbar. For a description of the parameters, see the comments for the constructor.

It is often useful to call this method if the user resizes the page, since that would change the *visible* parameter. You should also call this method if the amount of data being displayed changes (e.g., if the user adds or removes data).

SecurityManager (lang)

There is always one of these objects, which you can obtain a reference to with System.getSecurityManager. Normal applications would not do so. Only programs like Web browsers need its methods.

SequenceInputStream (io)

This is a perfectly ordinary InputStream, except for the fact that it allows you to treat several streams as one long stream. As the data from the first stream is exhausted, the *read* method simply switches to the next stream. The *read* method will continue returning data until all the streams are exhausted.

```
public SequenceInputStream(InputStream s1, InputStream s2);
public SequenceInputStream(Enumeration e);
```

These methods allow you to create an object of the SequenceInputStream class.

The first constructor creates a SequenceInputStream which consists of only two InputStreams.

The second constructor creates a SequenceInputStream which can consist of any number of InputStreams. To use the second constructor, you must create a sub-class of the Enumeration class. This sub-class would have a *nextElement* method that returns the next InputStream that will be used by the SequenceInputStream.

```
public int read() throws IOException;
public int read(byte bytes[]) throws IOException;
public int read(byte bytes[], int offset, int length) throws IOException;
```

These methods let you read data from the stream. The first method reads a single byte. The second method reads up to *b.length* bytes into array *b*. The third reads up to *length* bytes into array *b* starting at index offset. The second and third methods return the number of bytes actually read. They will all return -1 if the end of the stream is reached before any data is read.

```
public int available() throws IOException;
```

This method tells you how many bytes of data can be read from the stream without waiting for a disk or network read operation.

```
public void close() throws IOException;
```

This method will close the stream.

```
public long skip(long n) throws IOException;
```

This method will skip past the next *n* bytes in the stream. It will return the number of bytes skipped.

ServerSocket (net)

This class can be used by a server to get new connections to clients. It is used behind the scenes by other Java classes; you would only use it if you were performing low-level Internet communications yourself.

```
public ServerSocket(int port) throws IOException;
public ServerSocket(int port, int count) throws IOException;
public InetAddress getInetAddress();
public int getLocalPort();
public Socket accept() throws IOException;
public void close() throws IOException;
public String toString();
public static synchronized void setSocketFactory(SocketImplFactory fac) throws ⇐
IOException;
```

169

Socket (net)

This class provides sockets, which are used to communicate over the Internet. It is used behind the scenes by other Java classes; you would only use it if you were performing low-level Internet communications yourself.

```
public Socket(String host, int port) throws UnknownHostException, IOException;
public Socket(String host, int port, boolean stream) throws IOException;
public Socket(InetAddress address, int port) throws IOException;
public Socket(InetAddress address, int port, boolean stream) throws IOException;
public InetAddress getInetAddress();
public int getPort();
public int getLocalPort();
public InputStream getInputStream() throws IOException;
public OutputStream getOutputStream() throws IOException;
public synchronized void close() throws IOException;
public String toString();
public static synchronized void setSocketImplFactory(SocketImplFactory fac) throws ⇐
IOException;
```

Stack (util)

This class lets you create a stack of objects. This stack operates just like a stack of dishes—the last item you put on the stack will be the first one you take off.

`public Stack();`

These constructors allow you to create objects of the Stack class.

`public Object push(Object item);`

This lets you add a new object to the top of the stack.

`public Object pop();`

This removes the object from the top of the stack. The removed object is returned by the method. If the stack is empty, an EmptyStackException will be thrown.

`public Object peek();`

This method returns the object which is on the top of the stack, but does not remove it from the stack. If the stack is empty, an EmptyStackException will be thrown.

`public boolean empty();`

This method returns true if the stack has no objects on it.

`public int search(Object o);`

This method searches the stack for the given object. If it is found, the method returns its index within the stack. (For example, it would return zero if the object were on the top of the stack.) If it isn't found, -1 is returned.

StreamTokenizer (io)

This class allows you to read data from a stream in the form of tokens. A token is a string of characters, and each token in the stream is separated from the next token by a special character. For example, if you decide that a comma is a separation character, then a stream with the data *aaa,b,c* would have five tokens: *aaa*, comma, *b*, comma, and *c*. This class would allow you to read those tokens, one at a time.

The key method in the class is nextToken, which will obtain the next token from the stream. The token is returned in two parts. The first part is the token itself, which is returned in sval and nval. Use sval to contain the token if it isn't a number, and nval to contain the token if it is a number. Neither will have a value if the token is a special character (such as a comma).

The second part of the token is ttype, which indicates what type of token it is. It will be TT_EOF for an end of file, TT_EOL for an end of line, TT_NUMBER if the token is a number (in which case, it will be in nval), and TT_WORD if the token is a String (in which case, it will be in sval). If the token is a special character, ttype will contain that character, sval will be null, and nval will be zero.

Before you call *nextToken* for the first time, you would normally use several of the other methods in the class (such as *wordChars*) to indicate the rules that should be followed in breaking the stream into tokens. By default, the following rules will apply:

■ Any character which isn't a letter or a digit is a special character. These characters separate tokens.

■ Any character with a value less than or equal to 32 (a space) will be considered a whitespace character.

■ A '/' character begins a comment, and the comment is ended at the end of the line.

■ Both single and double quotes (' and ") are quote characters. When one is encountered, everything up to the matching quote is considered to be one token.

```
public static final int TT_EOF;
public static final int TT_EOL;
public static final int TT_NUMBER;
public static final int TT_WORD;
```

These are the special values ttype can have to indicate a special kind of token.

```
public int ttype;
```

This field variable indicates the type of the current token. It can have one of the four special values listed above, or it can be the special character that acted as a token separator.

```
public String sval;
public double nval;
```

These field variables contain the token itself. If the token is numeric, ttype will be set to TT_NUMBER, and the token will be placed in nval. If the token is a string, ttype will be set to TT_WORD, and the token will be placed in sval.

```
public StreamTokenizer (InputStream in);
```

This constructor allows you to create a StreamTokenizer object. The *in* stream will be used to obtain the raw characters to be broken into tokens.

```
public void resetSyntax();
```

This removes all the current processing rules, and changes to a simple set of rules. Those simple rules are that every character is a special character, and thus will terminate a token. (After calling this method to clear things, you would normally call some of the other methods to put new rules in effect.)

```
public void wordChars(int low, int hi);
public void whitespaceChars(int low, int hi);
public void ordinaryChars(int low, int hi);
public void ordinaryChar(int ch);
public void commentChar(int ch);
public void slashStarComments(boolean flag);
public void slashSlashComments(boolean flag);
public void quoteChar(int ch);
public void parseNumbers();
public void eolIsSignificant(boolean flag);
public void lowerCaseMode(boolean fl);
```

171

These are the methods you can use to alter the set of rules used to break the stream into tokens.

The first four methods specify character values that are to be considered a certain kind of character. Characters that are part of words are specified by *wordChars*. (You would often want letters to be in this category, and might want many other characters in it as well.) Characters that consistitute whitespace are specified by *whitespaceChars*. These characters are never returned in ttype, but they can still separate one token from another if there are no other special characters between two words. To separate words, the characters *ordinaryChar* and *ordinaryChars* are used, and are tokens by themselves. Characters such as ',' are often included in this category.

To specify a character that will begin a comment, use *commentCha*. This sort of comment will be ended by the end of line. You can also use *slashStarComment* to turn on a feature which causes text beginning with "/*" and ending with "*/" to be considered a comment, or you can use *slashSlashComments* to turn on a feature which causes text following "//" up to the end of the line to be a comment.

To specify a character that delimits strings, use *quoteChar*. For example, if you use *quoteChar*('\"'), then any series of characters beginning and ending with a quote (") will be considered one token.

parseNumbers turns on a feature which will put numeric values in *nval*. This feature is turned on by default, and can only be turned off by calling *resetSyntax*.

To turn on and off a feature that will consider end-of-line characters to be token separators, use *eolIsSignificant*. If this feature is off, end-of-line characters are treated like whitespace.

To turn on and off a feature which will convert all the letters in a token to lower case before placing it in sval use *lowerCaseMode*.

```
public int nextToken() throws IOException;
```

This method obtains the next token in the stream. It will place the token in sval or nval, and will put the type of token in ttype. That type will either be a character value (which means a special character was encountered in the stream) or one of the special TT constants. The method will return the same value placed in ttype.

```
public void pushBack();
```

This method will put the current token back onto the stream, so the next call to *nextToken* will return the same token again.

```
public int lineno();
```

This method returns the number of the line of text currently being processed.

```
public String toString();
```

This will convert the StreamTokenizer object to a String. This can be helpful in debugging a program, especially if the String is then passed to System.out.println.

String (lang)

Objects of this class are immutable. That means they are assigned a value when they are created, and that value cannot be changed later. If you want the object to have a different value, you must create a new object with that new value.

The indexes used in the methods in this class always start at zero. So, to reference the first character in the string, you use an index of zero. To reference the second character, you use an index of one. And so on. (Note the variation used by the *substring* method.)

```
public String();
public String(String value);
public String(char value[]);
public String(char value[], int offset, int count);
public String(byte ascii[], int hibyte, int offset, int count);
public String(byte ascii[], int hibyte);
public String (StringBuffer buffer);
```

These constructors let you create a String object. The *offset* parameter is the index of the first element of the array to use. The *count* parameter is the number of elements in the array to use. The *hibyte* parameter is the value to use for the high-order byte of the Unicode character. (You would normally use zero for this.)

```
public int length();
```

This returns the number of characters in the String.

```
public char charAt(int index);
```

This returns the character at the specified index.

```
public void getChars(int srcBegin, int srcEnd, char dst[], int dstBegin);
public void getBytes(int srcBegin, int srcEnd, byte dst[], int dstBegin);
```

These methods let you extract part of the String into a char or byte array. The *srcBegin* and *srcEnd* parameters specify the beginning and ending indexes in the String that should be copied. The *dstBegin* indicates the first index of the array into which characters will be copied.

```
public boolean equals(Object anObject);
public boolean equalsIgnoreCase(String anotherString);
public int compareTo(String anotherString);
```

These methods compare two strings. The first one returns true if they match. The second method returns true if they match, but doesn't consider case differences. The third method returns a value that is less than zero if the String object is less than the *String* parameter; it returns zero if the two Strings are equal; and it returns a value that is greater than zero if the String object is greater than the *String* parameter.

```
public boolean regionMatches(int myOffset, String other, int otherOffset, int len);
public boolean regionMatches(boolean ignoreCase, int myOffset, String other, ⇐
int otherOffset, int len);
```

173

These methods compare parts of two Strings. They return true if the two parts match. The *myOffset* parameter specifies the index to start the comparison in the String object. The *other* parameter is the other string to compare to. The comparison will start at index *otherOffset* in that string. The comparison will involve len characters. You can set *ignoreCase* to true if you want the comparison to be done without regard to the case of the characters.

```
public boolean startsWith(String prefix, int toffset);
public boolean startsWith(String prefix);
public boolean endsWith(String suffix);
```

These methods return true if the String begins or ends with a specified prefix or suffix. The *toffset* parameter specifies the starting index in the String object to use for the comparison.

```
public int indexOf(int ch);
public int indexOf(int ch, int fromIndex);
public int lastIndexOf(int ch);
public int lastIndexOf(int ch, int fromIndex);
public int indexOf(String str);
public int indexOf(String str, int fromIndex);
public int lastIndexOf(String str);
public int lastIndexOf(String str, int fromIndex);
```

These methods determine the index, if any, at which a given character or string exists within the String object. The *fromIndex* parameter indicates the first index at which the search should be made. The methods beginning with last will find the last occurrence of the string or character; the others will find the first occurrence. The methods return -1 if the character or string is not found.

```
public String substring(int beginIndex);
public String substring(int beginIndex, int endIndex);
```

These methods create a new String object which is a substring of the original String object. The *beginIndex* is the index at which the substring begins, and the *endIndex* parameter is one higher than the index at which the substring ends. Thus, substring(4,5) returns a String with just one character—the character at index 4.

The second version of the method creates a substring beginning at *beginIndex* and ending at the end of the string.

```
public String concat(String str);
```

This method returns a new string which consists of the old String object concatenated with the str.

```
public String replace(char oldChar, char newChar);
```

This method creates a new string in which every occurrence of *oldChar* is replaced with *newChar*.

```
public String toLowerCase();
public String toUpperCase();
```

These methods create a new string in which all the characters have been converted to upper- or lowercase.

```
public String trim();
```

This method creates a new String in which all the leading and trailing whitespace has been removed.

```
public String toString();
```

Yes, that's right—this method returns the object you call it with.

```
public char[] toCharArray();
```

This method creates a char array, and puts the contents of the String in the array.

```
public static String valueOf(char data[]);
public static String valueOf(char data[], int offset, int count);
public static String copyValueOf(char data[], int offset, int count);
public static String copyValueOf(char data[]);
```

These methods create a new String object from an array of *char*. The *offset* parameter specifies the first index in the array that is to be used in the String. The *count* parameter specifies the number of characters to be used in the String. If *offset* and *count* are not used, the entire array will be used in the String.

The difference between the first two methods and the second two methods is a bit tricky. You see, a String object uses an array of char to store the characters. (Of course, you can't access that array directly, but it's still there.) If you use the first two methods, they will use your original array for the new String object. If you use one of the second two methods, it will make a copy of the array, and use that copy. Which you do will often not matter, but if you plan on making further changes to the array, you should watch out, because that will also modify the String object if you use the first two methods.

175

```
public static String valueOf(Object obj);
public static String valueOf(boolean b);
public static String valueOf(char c);
public static String valueOf(int i);
public static String valueOf(long l);
public static String valueOf(float f);
public static String valueOf(double d);
```

These methods will convert various data types to a new String object.

StringBuffer (lang)

This class is similar to the String class, but it is not immutable; that is, objects of the StringBuffer class can be changed.

Although there are some methods in this class which allow you to effect the amount of storage reserved to hold the String (such as the second version of the constructor), you don't generally need to worry about that. If you add additional characters to the String (e.g., by calling append), additional storage space will be obtained if necessary.

Many of the methods in this class use an index to specify a certain location within the String. This index is always zero-based. This means you use a value of zero to reference the first character, a value of one to reference the second character, and so on.

```
public StringBuffer();
public StringBuffer(int length);
public StringBuffer(String str);
```

These constructors let you create a StringBuffer object. The first version creates an empty String. The second also creates an empty String, but reserves enough space to hold length characters. The third version creates a String with the given value.

```
public int length();
```

This method returns the number of characters in the String.

```
public int capacity();
```

This method returns the number of characters which can be held in the storage space currently reserved by the object.

```
public synchronized void ensureCapacity(int minimumCapacity);
```

This will increase the storage space reserved by the object, if necessary, so it can hold at least minimumCapacity characters.

```
public synchronized void setLength(int newLength);
```

176

This method will set the length of the String to newLength characters. If newLength is less than the current length of the String, characters will be removed from the end of the String. If newLength is greater than the current length of the String, characters with a value of zero will be added to the end of the String.

```
public synchronized char charAt(int index);
```

This method returns the character at the given index.

```
public synchronized void getChars(int srcBegin, int srcEnd, char dst[], int dstBegin);
```

This method copies some (or all) of the characters from the String into a *char* array. The parameters *srcBegin* and *srcEnd* are the indexes of the String to copy. Since *srcEnd* is one greater than the last character to copy, if *srcBegin* is 2, and *srcEnd* is 3, the single character at index 2 will be copied. The characters will be copied to dst, beginning at index *dstBegin*.

```
public synchronized void setCharAt(int index, char ch);
```

This method sets the character at index to the value *ch*.

```
public synchronized StringBuffer append(Object obj);
public synchronized StringBuffer append(String str);
public synchronized StringBuffer append(char str[]);
public synchronized StringBuffer append(char str[], int offset, int len);
public StringBuffer append(boolean b);
public synchronized StringBuffer append(char c);
public StringBuffer append(int i);
```

```
public StringBuffer append(long l);
public StringBuffer append(float f);
public StringBuffer append(double d);
```

All these methods allow you to append a String to the end of the existing one. If the parameter is of a different type (such as an *int*), the parameter is converted to a String and then appended.

```
public synchronized StringBuffer insert(int offset, Object obj);
public synchronized StringBuffer insert(int offset, String str);
public synchronized StringBuffer insert(int offset, char str[]);
public StringBuffer insert(int offset, boolean b);
public synchronized StringBuffer insert(int offset, char c);
public StringBuffer insert(int offset, int i);
public StringBuffer insert(int offset, long l);
public StringBuffer insert(int offset, float f);
public StringBuffer insert(int offset, double d);
```

These methods allow you to insert new characters in the middle of the string. (The characters after the point of insertion are retained; they are simply shifted to the right.) The offset is the index at which the new characters will be inserted. Thus, if the offset is 2, all the characters which used to reside at index 2 and beyond will be moved following the newly added text.

```
public String toString();
```

This creates a new String object with the same contents as the StringBuffer.

StringBufferInputStream (io)

177

Streams generally represent disk files, but they don't have to. They can represent any series of characters. In the StringBufferInputStream, the stream represents a String object.

```
public StringBufferInputStream(String str);
```

This constructor lets you create objects of the StringBufferInputStream class. You must specify the String which holds the data to be used as the stream in str.

```
public synchronized int read();
public synchronized int read(byte b[]);
public synchronized int read(byte b[], int offset, int len);
```

These methods let you read from the stream. The first method will return a single byte from the stream. The second will read up to *b.length* bytes into array *b*. The third will read up to *len* characters from the stream, and put them in array *b* starting at offset. All three methods will return -1 if no bytes were read because the end of the stream was encountered.

```
public synchronized long skip(long n);
```

      This method lets you skip past *n* bytes of the stream. It returns the actual number of bytes skipped.

```
public synchronized int available();
```

      This method returns the number of bytes left in the stream.

```
public synchronized void reset();
```

      This method resets the processing to the beginning of the stream. (Following this, subsequent calls to *read* will obtain data from the beginning of the stream.)

```
public void close();
```

      This method closes the stream.

StringTokenizer (util)

      This method will let you break a String into a series of tokens or substrings. For example, if you had the String "abc,def;ghi", and you had defined both commas and semicolons to be delimiters, then the String would have the tokens "abc", "def", and "ghi".

```
public StringTokenizer(String str);
public StringTokenizer(String str, String delim);
public StringTokenizer(String str, String delim, boolean returnTokens);
```

      These constructors let you create a *StringTokenizer* object. The *str* is the String to be broken into tokens. The *delim* is a String which contains the characters which are valid delimiters. If true, *returnTokens* will cause the *nextToken* and *nextElement* methods to return delimiters as if they were tokens. If this is false, which is the default, delimiters are not returned by *nextToken* or *nextElement*.

      If you don't specify a *delim* parameter, the default will be a string containing a space, tab, return, and new line.

```
public boolean hasMoreTokens();
public boolean hasMoreElements();
```

      These methods perform the same function. They return true if there is at least one more token in the String.

```
public String nextToken();
public String nextToken(String delim);
public Object nextElement();
```

      These methods all return the next token in the String. If there are no more tokens, a NoSuchElementException will be thrown.

      If you specify *delim*, the tokenizer will switch to it as the list of delimiters. (The switch takes place before the next token is located.)

```
public int countTokens();
```

      This method will return the number of tokens in the String.

System (lang)

This class provides methods which allow you to perform various system-level tasks. For example, it includes three stream *variables*, *System.in*, *System.out*, and *System.err*, which allow you to read from the keyboard and write to the screen.

All of the methods in this class are static, which means you never create an object of type System.

```
public static InputStream in;
public static PrintStream out;
public static PrintStream err;
```

These field variables provide streams you can use to read from the keyboard and write to the screen. In a GUI environment, such as Windows, these have limited value, but can still be useful. For example, using System.out.println can be a convenient way of displaying debugging information during program development.

```
public static native long currentTimeMillis();
```

This method returns the number of milliseconds since January 1, 1970. (This is a convenient time-reporting mechanism since you can easily use it to create an object of the Date class.)

```
public static native void arraycopy(Object src, int src_position, Object dst, ⇐
int dst_position, int length);
```

This will copy elements from the *src* array to the *dst* array. The copying will begin at index *src_position* in *src,* and begin at index *dst_position* in *dst.* The number of elements copied will be *length.* This method will work with arrays of any type of object, although both *src* and *dst* should be of the same type. This method doesn't allocate space for *dst*— you should do that before calling the method.

179

```
public static Properties getProperties();
public static void setProperties(Properties props);
public static String getProperty(String key);
public static String getProperty(String key, String def);
```

These methods allow you to access the system properties. The last two methods are the most useful, because they allow you to specify the key of the property to be obtained. Although other keys may be available, the ones shown in Table 7-2 will always be available.

Table 7-2 System properties

Key	Description
java.version	The Java version number.
java.vendor	The Java vendor.
java.vendor.url	The URL for the Java vendor.

continued on next page

continued from previous page

Key	Description
java.home	The Java installation directory.
java.class.version	The version number of the Java classes.
java.class.path	The Java classpath.
os.name	The operating system name.
os.arch	The operating system architecture.
os.version	The operating system version.
file.separator	The separator used between directory names in a pathname.
path.separator	The separator used between pathnames in a list of pathnames.
line.separator	The normal end-of-line character sequence.
user.name	User account name.
user.home	User home directory.
user.idr	The user's current working directory.

180

```
public static void exit (int status);
public static void gc();
public static void runFinalization();
public static void load(String filename);
public static void loadLibrary(String libname);
```

These methods are shortcuts to calling the same methods in the Runtime class. (See the Runtime class for their descriptions.)

Text Area(AWT)

TextArea objects let you create controls that allow entry of several lines of text.

TextArea is a sub-class of both TextComponent and Component, so you can use any of the *TextComponent* and *Component* methods on a TextArea object.

```
public TextArea();
public TextArea(int rows, int cols);
public TextArea(String text);
public TextArea(String text, int rows, int cols);
```

This constructors create a text area control. The second and third versions create a control which is *rows* high and *cols* wide (using average character widths). These are often the best versions to use if you want to insure that a certain amount of text will be visible in the control. Otherwise, the control can be resized by the layout manager.

The *text* parameter specifies the initial text to be displayed. If you want the text to cover more than one line of the control, you must insert \r characters in *text* to delimit the lines. (Otherwise, all the text will be displayed on the first line.)

```
public void insertText(String str, int pos);
public void appendText(String str);
public void replaceText(String str, int start, int end);
```

These methods let you change the text in the control. The positions (*pos*, *start*, and *end*) should be zero for the first character, one for the second, and so on.

```
public int getRows();
public int getColumns();
```

These methods let you get the values passed for *row* and *cols* to the constructor.

TextComponent (AWT)

You cannot create objects of this type. However, TextField and TextArea objects are subclasses of TextComponent, so you can use the methods of this class on those objects.

```
public void setText(String t);
public String getText();
public String getSelectedText()
```

These methods let you set or get the text in the control. The *getText* method gets all the text, while the *getSelectedText* method gets only the part of the text that is currently selected (highlighted). If no text is selected, *getSelectedText* will return a String with no characters.

```
public boolean isEditable();
public void setEditable(boolean t);
```

By default, TextArea and TextField controls can be edited by the user. You can turn that ability on and off using setEditable. You can use isEditable to find out whether that ability is on or off.

```
public int getSelectionStart();
public int getSelectionEnd();
```

These methods let you determine what portion of the text is selected (i.e., highlighted). The methods return indexes that will be zero if the first character is selected, one if the second is selected, etc.

```
public void select(int selStart, int selEnd);
public void selectAll();
```

These methods let you select (i.e., highlight) all or part of the text. The first method uses the selStart and selEnd indexes, which identify which characters should be selected. For example, select(1,2) would select the second and third characters.

TextField (AWT)

TextField objects let you create controls that allow the user to enter a line of text.

TextField is a sub-class of both *TextComponent* and *Component*, so you can use any of the *TextComponent* and *Component* methods on a TextField object.

```
public TextField();
public TextField(int cols);
public TextField(String text);
public TextField(String text, int cols);
```

These constructors let you create a TextField object. The second and fourth versions let you specify the width of the control, which is generally a good thing to do—otherwise, the layout manager will be able to change the size of the control.

```
public char getEchoChar();
public boolean echoCharIsSet();
public void setEchoCharacter(char c);
```

These methods let you set the echo character for the control. If you set a character as the echo character, then it will appear on the screen in place of each character typed by the user. Your program can still use getText to get the actual text that was typed. This is useful for password fields, because it prevents someone from reading the password from the screen.

```
public Dimension preferredSize(int cols);
public Dimension preferredSize();
public Dimension minimumSize(int cols);
public Dimension minimumSize();
```

These methods let you determine how large the control will be. The methods with the *cols* parameter give you information about the size the control would be if it were the specified number of columns in width. The other methods give information about the size based on the number of columns specified in the constructor.

Thread (lang)

The Thread class allows you to create a separate point of execution within the same program. To create a new thread, create a sub-class of Thread which overrides the *run* method. This method will contain the code you want to execute in the separate thread. Then, create an object of the new sub-class, and use the *start* method on it. The new thread can terminate itself either by returning from the *run* method or by calling the *stop* method.

Each thread is in a group of threads, represented by a ThreadGroup object. You can use the ThreadGroup object to perform certain operations on all the threads in the group.

```
public final static int MIN_PRIORITY;
public final static int NORM_PRIORITY;
public final static int MAX_PRIORITY;
```

These constants give some of the priority values that can be assigned to threads.

```
public Thread();
public Thread(Runnable target);
public Thread(ThreadGroup group, Runnable target);
public Thread(String name);
public Thread(ThreadGroup group, String name);
public Thread(Runnable target, String name);
public Thread(ThreadGroup group, Runnable target, String name);
```

These constructors let you create Thread objects.

If you specify a *target* parameter, that object must have a *run* method, and it is that method that will be activated when the *start* method is called. Otherwise, you should have sub-classed the Thread class, and the object of that sub-class will be the one activated.

If you wish, you can put the new thread in a group by specifying group, or give it a name by specifying name. Neither is useful in most situations. If you don't specify a group, Java will put it in a main group.

```
public synchronized native void start();
```

Calling this method will cause the *run* method for the new thread to be activated. Since *run* will be in a different thread than the one that called *start*, the *start* method can return to its caller, and that thread can continue running without having to wait for *run* to complete.

```
public void run();
```

If you sub-class the Thread class, you will normally provide an override for this method. It will be called when the thread is activated by calling the *start* method.

```
public final void stop();
```

The new thread can be stopped by calling this method. (It can be called either by the new thread itself, or by the thread that created it.)

```
public final native boolean isAlive();
```

This method returns true if the thread has been activated (by calling *start*), but has not yet finished (either by returning from the *run* method or by calling *stop*).

```
public final void suspend();
public final void resume();
```

The execution of the thread can be temporarily suspended by calling *suspend*. Once that is done, execution can be resumed by calling *resume*.

```
public final void setPriority(int newPriority);
public final int getPriority();
```

These methods let you get and set the priority for the thread. Although you can pass any numeric value, it must be at least Thread.MIN_PRIORITY and not more than Thread.MAX_PRIORITY.

```
public final void setName(String name);
public final String getName();
```

These methods let you set and get the name of the thread. The name can also be set in the constructor.

```
public final ThreadGroup getThreadGroup();
```

This method obtains the ThreadGroup object for the group the thread belongs to.

```
public static int activeCount();
```

This method returns the number of threads in the thread's group which are active.

```
public static int enumerate(Thread tarray[]);
```

This method puts in *tarray* a list of all the active Thread objects in the current group. The method returns the number of Thread objects put in the array.

```
public final synchronized void join(long millis) throws InterruptedException;
public final synchronized void join(long millis, int nanos) throws InterruptedException;
public final void join() throws InterruptedException;
```

This method will wait until the thread ends, or until *millis* milliseconds of time has passed. (If you want to provide the time more accurately, you can add an additional *nanos* nanoseconds.)

```
public final void setDaemon(boolean on);
public final boolean isDaemon();
```

A thread can be flagged as a daemon thread by calling setDaemon. You can determine if the thread has been flagged as a daemon with isDaemon.

A daemon thread operates just as an ordinary thread does. The only difference is that the Java virtual machine will exit as soon as all threads have completed except those marked as daemons. So, if you flag a thread as a daemon, you're telling Java it doesn't have to wait for the thread to finish before it exits.

Note that the meaning of daemon for threads is different than it is for thread groups.

```
public static native Thread currentThread();
```

This method returns the Thread object for the thread that calls it.

```
public static native void yield();
```

This method stops execution of the thread to allow other threads to execute. After the other threads have had a chance to run, the original thread will resume execution.

```
public static native void sleep(long millis) throws InterruptedException;
public static void sleep(long millis, int nanos) throws InterruptedException;
```

These methods cause the thread to stop executing for *millis* milliseconds plus *nanos* nanoseconds.

```
public void checkAccess();
```

This method checks to see if you have the necessary security authorization to control the thread. If you do, the method simply returns. If you don't, it will throw a SecurityException.

```
public String toString();
```

This will convert the Thread object to a String. This can be helpful in debugging a program, especially if the String is then passed to System.out.println.

ThreadGroup (lang)

Each Thread object belongs to a group which is represented by a ThreadGroup object. The ThreadGroup object allows you to perform certain operations on all the threads in the group.

```
public ThreadGroup(String name);
public ThreadGroup(ThreadGroup parent, String name);
```

These methods allow you to create a ThreadGroup object. The parent specifies the group that is to be the parent of the new group. All groups have a parent, except for the special system group which is at the root of the thread group tree. If you don't specify a parent, the parent of the group the calling thread belongs to will be the parent of the new group.

Each group has a name, but it has no effect on the way the group operates.

```
public final String getName();
```

This method returns the name of the group (which was specified when the constructor was called).

```
public final ThreadGroup getParent();
```

This method obtains the parent of the group. (Every group has a parent except the special system group.)

```
public final boolean parentOf(ThreadGroup g);
```

This method returns true if *g* is a parent of the group (either directly or indirectly). It will also return true if the two groups are the same.

```
public final int getMaxPriority();
public final synchronized void setMaxPriority(int pri);
```

These methods let you set and get the maximum priority any thread in the group is allowed to have.

```
public final boolean isDaemon();
public final void setDaemon(boolean daemon);
```

This lets you set and get the daemon flag. This flag indicates whether or not the group is a daemon group. A daemon group acts just like a regular group except that it will automatically be destroyed if the last thread in the group ends.

Note that the meaning of daemon for groups is different than that for individual threads.

```
public final void checkAccess();
```

This method checks to see if you have the authority to control the group. If you do, the method simply returns. If you don't, it throws a SecurityException.

```
public synchronized int activeCount();
```

This returns the number of active threads in the group. To be active a thread must have been started, but not yet stopped.

```
public int enumerate(Thread list[]);
public int enumerate(Thread list[], boolean recurse);
```

These methods put a list of all the Thread objects for the group into list. It returns the number of threads it put in list.

If recurse is true, the method will also process all the threads in the children of the current group (and their children, and so on).

```
public synchronized int activeGroupCount();
```

This method returns the number of thread groups in this thread group (i.e., the groups that are children of this group).

```
public int enumerate(ThreadGroup list[]);
public int enumerate(ThreadGroup list[], boolean recurse);
```

These methods put a list of all the ThreadGroup objects which are children of the group into list. It returns the number of objects put in list.

If recurse is true, it will also process all thread groups that are grandchildren, great grandchildren, and so on.

```
public final synchronized void stop();
```

This method will stop all the threads in the group.

```
public final synchronized void suspend();
public final synchronized void resume();
```

The *suspend* method will temporarily stop execution of all the threads in the group. You can later resume that execution with *resume*.

```
public final synchronized void destroy();
```

This method will destroy the thread group. This can only be done if all the threads in the group have already stopped.

```
public String toString();
```

This will convert the Thread object to a String. This can be helpful in debugging a program, especially if the String is then passed to System.out.println.

URL (net)

This is the only class in the net package which would be used by ordinary programs—those that are not trying to do their own low-level Internet communications.

Objects of this class represent the URL address of a file on the Internet.

```
public URL(String spec) throws MalformedURLException;
public URL(URL context, String spec) throws MalformedURLException;
```

These constructors let you create URL objects. The first form requires the complete URL address of the file. The second form can use a relative name, and the system will look for the name in the context. The context would normally be getDocumentBase() or getCodeBase(), from the Applet class.

```
public final InputStream openStream();
```

This method allows you to create an InputStream object which can be used to read the contents of the URL-specified file. (If the file is a .gif file you plan to display on the screen, you would normally use the *getImage* method in the Applet class instead of this method.)

```
public URL(String protocol, String host, int port, String file) throws ⇐
MalformedURLException;
public URL(String protocol, String host, String file) throws MalformedURLException;
public int getPort();
public String getProtocol();
public String getHost();
public String getFile();
public String getRef();
public boolean equals(Object obj);
boolean hostsEqual(String h1, String h2);
public boolean sameFile(URL other);
public String toString();
public String toExternalForm();
public URLConnection openConnection() throws java.io.IOException;
public final Object getContent();
public static synchronized void setURLStreamHandlerFactory(URLStreamHandlerFactory fac);
```

These methods are useful only if you are performing low-level Internet communications processing, which is not necessary for most programs.

URLConnection (net)

This class represents a connection over the Internet to a file described by an URL address. This class is used behind the scenes by Java, and you would not normally use it unless you were performing low-level Internet communcations processing.

```
public void connect() throws IOException;
public URL getURL();
public int getContentLength();
public String getContentType();
```

continued on next page

187

continued from previous page

```
public String getContentEncoding();
public long getExpiration();
public long getDate();
public long getLastModified();
public String getHeaderField(String name);
public int getHeaderFieldInt(String name, int Default);
public long getHeaderFieldDate(String name, long Default);
public String getHeaderFieldKey(int n);
public String getHeaderField(int n);
public Object getContent() throws IOException;
public InputStream getInputStream() throws IOException;
public OutputStream getOutputStream() throws IOException;
public String toString();
public void setDoInput(boolean doinput);
public void setDoOutput(boolean dooutput);
public void setAllowUserInteraction(boolean allowuserinteraction);
public static void setDefaultAllowUserInteraction(boolean defaultallowuserinteraction);
public void setUseCaches(boolean usecaches);
public boolean getDefaultUseCaches();
public void setRequestProperty(String key, String value);
public static void setDefaultRequestProperty(String key, String value);
public static String getDefaultRequestProperty(String key);
public static synchronized void setContentHandlerFactory(ContentHandlerFactory fac);
```

URLEncoder (net)

This class allows you to convert a string into the proper form for use as URL (i.e., spaces are replaced by "+", etc.) This class is used behind the scenes by Java, and you would not normally use it unless you were performing low-level Internet communications processing.

```
public static String encode(String s);
```

Vector (util)

The Vector class lets you create an indexed series of values, very much as an array does. Unlike an array, a Vector will grow as necessary when new elements are added.

Like an array, each object in a Vector is identified by an index. The first object has index zero, the second has index one, and so on.

```
public Vector();
public Vector(int initialCapacity);
public Vector(int initialCapacity, int capacityIncrement);
```

These constructors let you create a Vector object. The initialCapacity indicates how much storage space to reserve for elements of the vector. You need not worry too much about this, since the vector will grow as needed when new elements are added. The capacityIncrement is the number of elements to be added to the storage space for the vector when new space is needed. If you don't supply initialCapacity or capacityIncrement, default values will be used.

```
public final synchronized void copyInto(Object anArray[]);
```

This copies the objects from the vector into an array.

```
public final synchronized void trimToSize();
```

This method removes any excess space. Excess space is space which has been reserved for the vector, but which is not currently being used.

```
public final synchronized void ensureCapacity(int minCapacity);
public final synchronized void setSize(int newSize);
```

To increase the space reserved for the vector use ensureCapacity, if necessary, so it has enough to hold minCapacity items. To change the space reserved for the vector use setSize so it will hold newSize objects (which might increase or decrease the space reserved).

```
public final int capacity();
public final int size();
```

At its current storage allocation, capacity returns the number of objects the vector can hold, and size returns the actual number of objects the vector currently has.

```
public final boolean isEmpty();
```

This returns true if there are currently no elements in the vector.

189

```
public final synchronized Enumeration elements();
```

This method will create an Enumeration object which will let you go through all the elements in the vector, one at a time.

```
public final boolean contains(Object elem);
```

This method returns true if the specified object is in the vector.

```
public final int indexOf(Object elem);
public final synchronized int indexOf(Object elem, int index);
```

These methods will return the index within the vector that contains the object elem. If you specify index, it will start looking for the object at that index. If the object isn't found, -1 is returned.

```
public final int lastIndexOf(Object elem);
public final synchronized int lastIndexOf(Object elem, int index);
```

These methods search for the given object, just as *indexOf* does. The difference is that this method searches from the last object to the first, rather than from the first to the last.

```
public final synchronized Object elementAt(int index);
```

This method returns the object with the given index.

```
public final synchronized Object firstElement();
public final synchronized Object lastElement();
```

These methods return the first and last elements in the vector.

```
public final synchronized void setElementAt(Object obj, int index);
```

This method sets the element with the given index to be obj. This can only be used to replace an object which is already in the vector, not to add new items to the vector. In other words, there must already be an object at the given index.

```
public final synchronized void removeElementAt(int index);
```

This will remove the element at the given index from the vector. Elements which had been at higher indexes will be shifted down to fill in the empty space.

```
public final synchronized void insertElementAt(Object obj, int index);
```

This will insert a new element at the given index. If there are objects at that index or higher, they are shifted to higher indexes to make room.

```
public final synchronized void addElement(Object obj);
```

This method will add the specified object to the end of the vector.

```
public final synchronized boolean removeElement(Object obj);
```

This method will remove the specified object from the vector. It will return true if the element was found and removed. It will return false if the element wasn't found.

```
public final synchronized void removeAllElements();
```

This method will remove all the elements from the vector.

```
public synchronized Object clone();
```

This method will create a copy of the Vector. The new Vector object will contain the same objects as the old one (i.e., it will not create new element objects, just a new Vector object).

```
public String toString();
```

This will convert the Vector object to a String. This can be helpful in debugging a program, especially if the String is then passed to System.out.println.

Window (AWT)

This class is used internally by Java. Although you can create objects of this class, doing so would have little or no value in applications or applets. (If you want to create what a user would normally call a window, you want an object of the Frame class.)

This class is important mainly because it is a super-class of Dialog and Frame, and provides some important methods for them.

```
public Window(Frame parent);
```

This constructor lets you create Window objects.

```
public synchronized void pack();
```

After you have finished adding all the components to the dialog or frame, you should call this method. It will cause the layout manager to position the components within the dialog or frame.

```
public synchronized void show();
```

This method will cause the dialog or frame to become visible. (Remember that dialogs and frames are invisible by default, and will not become visible until you call this method.)

```
public synchronized void dispose();
```

Use this method to remove the dialog or frame from the screen.

```
public void toFront();
public void toBack();
```

Use this method to move the dialog or frame to the front or back of the stack of windows used by this application.

Index

Symbols

?: operator, 47
& (And) operator, 48
   compared to logical And (&&), 50-51
\ (backslash character), 46
/ (division) operator, 47
" (double-quote marks), 46
= (equal) operator, 50
== (equality) operator, 48
! (exclamation) operator, 47
^^ (exponent) operator, 48
> (greater than) operator, 48
>= (greater than or equal) operator, 48
| (inclusive or) operator, 48
< (left shift) operator, 49
< (less than) operator, 48
<= (less than or equal) operator, 48
&& (logical And) operator, 49
   compared to And (&) operator, 50-51
|| (logical or) operator, 49
* (multiplication) operator, 47
!= (not equal) operator, 48
% (percentage) operator, 47
+ (plus) operator, 47
++ (post fix addition) operator, 49
-- (post fix subtraction) operator, 49
>> (right shift) operator, 49
' (single-quote mark), 46
- (subtraction) operator, 47
~ (tilde) operator, 48
>>>(unsigned shift) operator, 50

A

Abstract keyword, 60, 62
access control, 67-68
Advanced language exercises, 11-12
And (&) operator, 48
   compared to logical And (&&) operator, 50-51
animation exercises, 10

applets (Java)
   defined, 57
   exercises, 9
applications, defined, 57
arrays, 54-55
   declaring, 69
   indexes, 54-55
   initializing, 70
   variables, 55
assignment statements, 71
AWT.Image package, 83
   ColorModel class, 100
   CropImageFilter class, 106
   DirectColorModel class, 112
   FilteredImageSource class, 122
   ImageConsumer class, 136
   ImageFilter class, 136
   ImageObserver class, 137
   ImageProducer class, 137
   IndexColorModel class, 137-138
   MemoryImageSource class, 148
   PixelGrabber class, 155
   RGBImageFilter class, 164-165
AWT package, 83
   BorderLayout class, 90-91
   Canvas class, 94-95
   CardLayout class, 95
   Checkbox class, 96-97
   CheckboxGroup class, 97
   CheckboxMenuItem class, 98
   Choice class, 98
   Color class, 99-100
   Component class, 101-104
   Container class, 104-105
   Dialog class, 111
   Dimension class, 111-112
   Event class, 114-116
   FileDialog class, 119-120*
   FlowLayout class, 124-125
   Font class, 125-126
   FontMetrics class, 126

193

195

197

199

NOTES

NOTES

NOTES

NOTES

NOTES

NOTES

NOTES

NOTES

NOTES

NOTES

Books have a substantial influence on the destruction of the forests of the Earth. For example, it takes 17 trees to produce one ton of paper. A first printing of 30,000 copies of a typical 480-page book consumes 108,000 pounds of paper, which will require 918 trees!

Waite Group Press™ is against the clear-cutting of forests and supports reforestation of the Pacific Northwest of the United States and Canada, where most of this paper comes from. As a publisher with several hundred thousand books sold each year, we feel an obligation to give back to the planet. We will therefore support organizations that seek to preserve the forests of planet Earth.

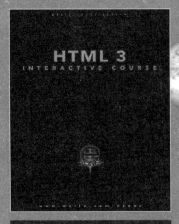

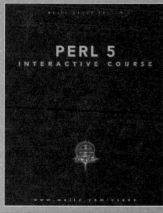

This is a legal agreement between you, the end user and purchaser, and The Waite Group®, Inc., and the authors of the programs contained in the disk. By opening the sealed disk package, you are agreeing to be bound by the terms of this Agreement. If you do not agree with the terms of this Agreement, promptly return the unopened disk package and the accompanying items (including the related book and other written material) to the place you obtained them for a refund.

SOFTWARE LICENSE

1. The Waite Group, Inc. grants you the right to use one copy of the enclosed software programs (the programs) on a single computer system (whether a single CPU, part of a licensed network, or a terminal connected to a single CPU). Each concurrent user of the program must have exclusive use of the related Waite Group, Inc. written materials.

2. The program, including the copyrights in each program, is owned by the respective author and the copyright in the entire work is owned by The Waite Group, Inc. and they are therefore protected under the copyright laws of the United States and other nations, under international treaties. You may make only one copy of the disk containing the programs exclusively for backup or archival purposes, or you may transfer the programs to one hard disk drive, using the original for backup or archival purposes. You may make no other copies of the programs, and you may make no copies of all or any part of the related Waite Group, Inc. written materials.

3. You may not rent or lease the programs, but you may transfer ownership of the programs and related written materials (including any and all updates and earlier versions) if you keep no copies of either, and if you make sure the transferee agrees to the terms of this license.

4. You may not decompile, reverse engineer, disassemble, copy, create a derivative work, or otherwise use the programs except as stated in this Agreement.

GOVERNING LAW

This Agreement is governed by the laws of the State of California.

LIMITED WARRANTY

The following warranties shall be effective for 90 days from the date of purchase: (i) The Waite Group, Inc. warrants the enclosed disk to be free of defects in materials and workmanship under normal use; and (ii) The Waite Group, Inc. warrants that the programs, unless modified by the purchaser, will substantially perform the functions described in the documentation provided by The Waite Group, Inc. when operated on the designated hardware and operating system. The Waite Group, Inc. does not warrant that the programs will meet purchaser's requirements or that operation of a program will be uninterrupted or error-free. The program warranty does not cover any program that has been altered or changed in any way by anyone other than The Waite Group, Inc. The Waite Group, Inc. is not responsible for problems caused by changes in the operating characteristics of computer hardware or computer operating systems that are made after the release of the programs, nor for problems in the interaction of the programs with each other or other software.

THESE WARRANTIES ARE EXCLUSIVE AND IN LIEU OF ALL OTHER WARRANTIES OF MERCHANTABILITY OR FITNESS FOR A PARTICULAR PURPOSE OR OF ANY OTHER WARRANTY, WHETHER EXPRESS OR IMPLIED.

EXCLUSIVE REMEDY

The Waite Group, Inc. will replace any defective disk without charge if the defective disk is returned to The Waite Group, Inc. within 90 days from date of purchase.

This is Purchaser's sole and exclusive remedy for any breach of warranty or claim for contract, tort, or damages.

LIMITATION OF LIABILITY

THE WAITE GROUP, INC. AND THE AUTHORS OF THE PROGRAMS SHALL NOT IN ANY CASE BE LIABLE FOR SPECIAL, INCIDENTAL, CONSEQUENTIAL, INDIRECT, OR OTHER SIMILAR DAMAGES ARISING FROM ANY BREACH OF THESE WARRANTIES EVEN IF THE WAITE GROUP, INC. OR ITS AGENT HAS BEEN ADVISED OF THE POSSIBILITY OF SUCH DAMAGES.

THE LIABILITY FOR DAMAGES OF THE WAITE GROUP, INC. AND THE AUTHORS OF THE PROGRAMS UNDER THIS AGREEMENT SHALL IN NO EVENT EXCEED THE PURCHASE PRICE PAID.

COMPLETE AGREEMENT

This Agreement constitutes the complete agreement between The Waite Group, Inc. and the authors of the programs, and you, the purchaser.

Some states do not allow the exclusion or limitation of implied warranties or liability for incidental or consequential damages, so the above exclusions or limitations may not apply to you. This limited warranty gives you specific legal rights; you may have others, which vary from state to state.

DIGITAL
CONNECTION™

About Digital Connection™

Digital Connection, a forward-thinking, leading-edge software development company based in New York City, is a premier developer of information technologies.

It has been integral in the development of major commercial online services, the Internet, and enterprise-wide systems for more than a decade. Digital Connection is a leader in graphical user interfaces, networking, object-oriented development, database technologies, and is a recognized pioneer in Java development.

Accomplishments range from multimedia games and complex financial systems to interactive videodisc kiosks and million-plus user online services.

The Digital Connection team possesses a unique combination of expertise in technology, business strategy, usability, and project management that translates into well-integrated, robust, high-impact solutions for its corporate clients.

Digital Connection is proud to have been technical consultant on *Talk Java to Me* for Waite Group Press™.

Digital Connection can be reached at:
http://www.digitalconnect.com
Digital Connection
372 Central Park West
New York, NY 10025
212.866.7000 (voice)
212.662.9560 (fax)
digital@pangaea.net

SATISFACTION REPORT CARD

Please fill out this card if you wish to know of future updates to
Talk Java to Me, or to receive our catalog.

First Name: _____ **Last Name:** _____

Street Address: _____

City: _____ **State:** _____ **Zip:** _____

E-Mail Address _____

Daytime Telephone: (   ) _____

Date product was acquired: Month_____ **Day**_____ **Year**_____ **Your Occupation:** _____

Overall, how would you rate *Talk Java to Me?*

☐ Excellent ☐ Very Good ☐ Good
☐ Fair ☐ Below Average ☐ Poor

What did you like MOST about this book? _____
_____
_____

What did you like LEAST about this book? _____
_____
_____

Please describe any problems you may have encountered with installing or using the disk: _____
_____

How did you use this book (problem-solver, tutorial, reference…)?
_____

What is your level of computer expertise?
☐ New ☐ Dabbler ☐ Hacker
☐ Power User ☐ Programmer ☐ Experienced Professional

What computer languages are you familiar with? _____
_____

Please describe your computer hardware:
Computer _____ Hard disk _____
5.25" disk drives _____ 3.5" disk drives _____
Video card _____ Monitor _____
Printer _____ Peripherals _____
Sound Board _____ CD ROM _____

Where did you buy this book?

☐ Bookstore (name): _____
☐ Discount store (name): _____
☐ Computer store (name): _____
☐ Catalog (name): _____
☐ Direct from WGP ☐ Other _____

What price did you pay for this book? _____

What influenced your purchase of this book?
☐ Recommendation ☐ Advertisement
☐ Magazine review ☐ Store display
☐ Mailing ☐ Book's format
☐ Reputation of Waite Group Press ☐ Other

How many computer books do you buy each year?_____

How many other Waite Group books do you own?_____

What is your favorite Waite Group book?_____
_____

Is there any program or subject you would like to see Waite Group Press cover in a similar approach?_____
_____

Additional comments?_____
_____
_____

Please send to: **Waite Group Press
200 Tamal Plaza
Corte Madera, CA 94925**

☐ **Check here for a free Waite Group catalog**

BEFORE YOU OPEN THE DISK OR CD-ROM PACKAGE ON THE FACING PAGE, CAREFULLY READ THE LICENSE AGREEMENT.

Opening this package indicates that you agree to abide by the license agreement found in the back of this book. If you do not agree with it, promptly return the unopened disk package (including the related book) to the place you obtained them for a refund.